Passing on the Passion
A Mother's Journey of Faith

Cricket Albertson

To order this book, go to www.cometothefire.org.

Library of Congress Cataloging in Publication Data:
ISBN 978-0-9838316-2-4
Printed in the United States of America

10 9 8 7 6 5 4 3 2 1

Table of Contents

For my Mama
Whose love for Jesus has never wavered
Whose joy in Jesus is always contagious and
Whose passion for sharing Jesus blesses all her children.

CHAPTER 1

Passing on the Passion

And He said to me, "It is done! I am the Alpha and the Omega, the Beginning and the End. I will give of the fountain of the water of life freely to him who thirsts. He who overcomes shall inherit all things, and I will be his God and he shall be My son" (Revelation 21:6-7).
Read Revelation 21.

On her deathbed, Catherine Booth said to her son Bramwell, "Try to raise up Christian mothers. Christian mothers are the want of the world."

This little volume has one purpose: to encourage Christian women and mothers who have a desire to pass on a passion for Christ to the next generation. This sacred trust of communicating our love for Christ to a new generation may be the most momentous issue of our time. In this day every sacred thing has been tarnished, and every hallowed place desecrated. The world needs the love of Christ manifested in the lives of believers through the power of the Holy Spirit.

Many times, the first generation of Christians has a passion for Christ, and they are deeply committed to following Him no matter the cost. The second generation of Christian believers becomes accustomed to grace, settle in comfortably, and live with low expectations for God's power. The third generation of Christians can be Christians in name only, following the family tradition rather than having a real relationship with the living Lord Jesus.

Passing on the passion for Christ from one generation to the next is the beautiful privilege of the people of God. This treasure that we possess is not a burden, not merely a responsibility, but a journey of joy. Isobel Kuhn in her book, *Ascent to the Tribes,* states it this way: "You can never give another person that which you have found spiritually but you can make him homesick for what you have." Creating a desire in our children for Christ comes out of the overflow of our love for Jesus and His Word.

How can we as Christians share with our children and our families a deep love and passionate commitment to Jesus Christ? How can the second and third generation slide be stopped? Passing on a passion for anything is never a formula. It is not a book to learn or something to do. It is about being a devoted and wholehearted follower of Jesus, a woman who loves Jesus Christ with all her heart, mind, soul and strength. Love is contagious, and only our love and devotion to Him will cause our children and grandchildren to want to follow Him.

Deuteronomy 6:4-9 shows that from the beginning God wanted his people to be passing on a passion and a love for him to their children. "Hear, O Israel: The Lord our God, the Lord is one! You shall love the Lord your God with all your heart, with all your soul, and with all your strength. And these words which I command you today shall be in your heart. You shall teach them diligently to your children, and you shall talk of them when you sit in your house, when you walk by the way, when you lie down, and when you rise up. You shall bind them as a sign on your hand, and they shall be as frontlets between your eyes. You shall write them on the doorposts of your house and on your gates."

How is passion communicated? Certainly not by formulas, rules or regulations. If we want to help the next generation fall in love with Christ, we must be passionate about Him ourselves. That ardor must continue unabated with freshness and openness and contentment.

Our children recognize stale faith, closed hearts and discontented spirits in their parents. They have no interest in religious drudgery nor should they. They will uncover any hypocrisy in us, and it will weaken their own faith. Passion for Jesus must be flourishing in us in order for it to be contagious and passed on to those whom God has entrusted to us.

Three-year-olds may be able to teach us the greatest lessons about God. One day I stopped by my sister's house just for a moment; her husband had recently come in from work and was sitting on the couch. Her three-year-old ran around the living room happily. When my nine-year-old daughter came through the door, the three-year-old began running from his daddy to his cousin, back and forth, calling out, "Daaaaady...Daaaaady...Daaaady."

At first, we were puzzled by what he was trying to communicate, and then we understood. He wanted his cousin to know that his daddy was home! The presence of the beloved father had to be celebrated by all who walked in the room, and the young son would run around calling out until recognition was given to his father.

Isn't that how God the Father would like us to feel about Him? Running around calling out his name until everyone we know recognizes His glory. Pure delight in his father caused this little child to want to share his joy. Pure delight in our heavenly Father will overflow in worship and in witness. In Psalm 27:4, David says, "One thing I have desired of the Lord, that I will seek after: That I may dwell in the house of the LORD all the days of my life, to behold the beauty of the LORD and to inquire in His temple." The New King James alternatively translates the word "beauty" as "delightfulness." Our Father wants to bring delight to our hearts as we live in His presence.

Passing on the passion to our children is an opportunity to pass on our delight in the Father and in our Savior. Not merely training our children or instilling godly character, however important those are, but living before them a delighted contentedness in the goodness of our God. The Psalmist captured the heart of this in Psalm 36. "How precious is Your lovingkindness, O God! Therefore the children of men put their trust under the shadow of Your wings. They are abundantly satisfied with the fullness of Your house, And you give them drink from the river of your pleasures. For with You is the fountain of life; in your light, we see light" (vss. 7-9).

A woman has a special role to play in passing on a passion for Christ to her children, her family and those God brings into her life. In a unique way, she becomes a mediator of the love and grace of Christ. When Christ lives in us, and His life flows out of our hearts, we stand between God's redeeming love and a world's need of it. Christian believers stand on the border of two worlds, between heaven and earth. We are pilgrims on earth and our true home is in heaven; we live with the door open to the eternal Father, and communication with God Himself happens every day, every moment. This eternal world cannot be seen or touched or measured, so all of us have to come to it through another way: through the lives of other people.

Because of Jesus, we become doorways through which other people can meet the risen Christ. When our lives are opportunities for others to meet Christ, our friends meet the risen Lord Jesus face to face. We are to live so that others can see Him through our lives and can be drawn into fellowship with Christ through the Holy Spirit in us. Paul's testimony as he says good-bye to the Ephesian church articulates this eternal calling God has given, "But my life is worth nothing to me unless I use it for finishing the work assigned me by the Lord Jesus, the work of telling others the good news about the wonderful grace of God" (Acts 20:24 NLT).

This little book is offered as encouragement to those in the throes of rearing children or loving children in Jesus' name and for His sake. God will give spiritual children to all His followers whether they are our physical children or not. It does not matter; we are to invest in the ones He gives to us so the next generation can know the Savior. Perhaps it will help all of us to know that we are not alone in the pursuit of God and in the desire to share His love and grace with our children.

The stories here may remind you of your own family's journey of faith, and it may give you courage to share your story with someone else. These are some of the lessons He has been teaching me in the midst of all the busyness of life as I have asked Jesus how to pass on a passion for Him to my children. My joy has been that He comes to meet me every time I cry out to Him, and He opens His Word to my heart in ways I can hear, understand and apply with my family.

A Quick Overview

Here is a quick overview of the lessons God is teaching me as I open my heart to Him and cry out to Him for wisdom and guidance and help. There are two of God's promises that I have been claiming as I seek His wisdom in how to share His wonderful goodness with my family.

"If any of you lacks wisdom let him ask of God who gives to all liberally and without reproach, and it will be given to him" (James 1:5). "Ask and it will be given to you; seek and you will find; knock and it will be opened to you. For everyone who asks receives, and he who seeks finds, and to him who knocks it will be opened" (Matthew 7:7-8).

The first lesson God is teaching me is that women have a special opportunity to be doors of grace for our children and our spheres of influence whether they be large or small. As we stand open to the Father and live in the presence of the Son through the power of the Holy Spirit, our families will be able to see through us into the presence of the Holy One.

In order to live as a doorway of grace, we have to make a million dollar gamble; we must give ourselves to God without any reservation. Like Ruth, we must abandon all we have known before and journey forward with courage and boldness, entrusting ourselves into the hands of our kinsman redeemer. Our courage to trust Him completely will create a secure place for our children to learn, grow and flourish.

God is also revealing that as we go forward with Christ, we must be sanctified and filled with His Holy Spirit. The indwelling Holy Spirit is not an extra or an add-on to the heart of God's good news; He is the one who lives in us and enables us to participate in God's life. His Spirit is the completion of who we were created to be, and the Spirit will bring life to us and to our families.

We have the holy privilege of believing that our children can also be filled with the Holy Spirit, set apart for Jesus Christ. Our children can know a freedom and joy in Christ which will prepare them for this adventure of faith and will help them live in Christ without guilt and condemnation. Romans 8:1 can be the motto of their lives. "There is therefore no condemnation for those who are in Christ Jesus who do not walk according to the flesh but according to the Spirit."

I am also learning that this freedom, joy and salvation are God's plan for his whole world. He wants every single boy and girl to know Christ and love Him, and as families we have the opportunity to be part of fulfilling God's purpose. Cornelius' encounter with God and then with Peter opens the door for the whole world to know Jesus. Our children can become part of God's redemptive story very early. "Out of the mouths of babes and nursing infants, you have ordained strength" (Psalm 8:20).

Sanctification is not the end of the spiritual journey; it is the beginning. Once we are living in the Spirit and claiming that joy for our children as well, we can move forward to claim the land and the inheritance God has given to us. We have nothing to lose as we cross the Jordan. As our children participate in this with us, they will know the thrill and joy of living a life of faith and dependence on Christ.

In the Promised Land, giants awaited the people of God. It will be the same for our families as we journey deeper, but Caleb and his daughter Achsah were not afraid of the giants and claimed their inheritance with boldness. We have the joy of beginning to teach our children how to face the giants that will come to meet them.

Ephesians 6 helps our children understand that they are warriors in this battle with a special role to fill, and they will be able to fight using the Word of God as their weapon. The Holy Spirit gives each child a special gift; mothers can encourage these God-given gifts to be used to help other people know Jesus personally. Encouragement is one of a mother's most important gifts to her children.

Finally, we rest in our Shepherd. He is the beginning and the end. The Shepherd and the doorway. As we rest contentedly in His presence, His peace and love can minister to those we love. The Hebrew of Luke 1:45 portrays this beautiful picture of believing in our God: "Blessed be the one believing because there shall be a completion to the things having been spoken to her from the Lord."

CHAPTER 2

Doors of Grace

"If anyone loves me, he will keep my word, and my Father will love him and we will come to him and make our home with him" (John 14:2-3).
Read Ephesians 3:16-21.

"Children tie the mother's feet," Amy Carmichael quotes this Tamil proverb in her book *Gold Cord*. Then she goes on to say, "Babies are truly a venture of faith and in India at least, they tie the mother's feet...we could not be too careful of our children's earliest years. So we let our feet be tied for love of Him whose feet were pierced." Children are a *venture of faith*; our faith increases as we trust the Father to help us love and train these ones He has entrusted to us. We have the solemn privilege of giving ourselves in love and prayer for these little ones. So we give ourselves to creating a home for God where our children can live joyfully and safely, where they can learn the truth about who He is and what He loves.

God must rejoice in the uniqueness of every family that belongs to him. As parents and followers of Jesus, we have the joy of creating a home that pleases God. The families do not need to all look the same because each disciple is different and special; each Spirit-led family will be one of a kind.

Each family has a role to fill in bringing God's kingdom to earth, and each child has a special mission, designed by God to fulfill. Every parent has a particular prayer burden and responsibility to create a space in the home for new followers of Jesus to be born, fed, nurtured and encouraged!

The most important single thing any parent can do is to fall in love with Jesus and be filled with His Holy Spirit. Then as life is lived daily, hourly, moment-by-moment, the Spirit will nudge each parent's heart about the needs of the children. The Holy Spirit becomes the primary player in the family, weaving together happy memories, times of encouragement, and building blocks for faith in Jesus that will enable the faith of the children to stand the test of time. This is the most important job we will ever do. Teaching our children to be disciples of Jesus, praying for them to be Christians in every sense of the word, and living Spirit-filled lives for them to see is our greatest privilege and joy.

"For this reason, I bow my knees to the Father of our Lord Jesus Christ, from whom the whole family in heaven and earth is named, that He would grant you, according to the riches of His glory to be strengthened with might through His Spirit in the inner man, that Christ may dwell in your hearts through faith, that you, being rooted and grounded in love, may be able to comprehend with all the saints what is the width, and length and depth and height – to know the love of Christ which passes knowledge; that you may be filled with all the fullness of God. Now unto Him who is able to do exceedingly abundantly above all that we ask or think, according to the power that works in us, to Him be glory in the church by Christ Jesus to all generations, forever and ever. Amen" (Eph. 3:14-21).

Being a Christian is like being an explorer. Just when you think you have discovered the greatest new land, you realize that there are spaces yet to be found and splendors yet to be seen. The more you explore and journey forward, the more you delight in and enjoy the grand vistas and hidden jewels. Paul's prayer for the Ephesian church is like buried treasure; the more you dig, the more gold you find. It is incredibly applicable to each Christian family.

This prayer is "to the Father of our Lord Jesus Christ, from whom the whole family is named." Every family is created in the image of the triune God; the oneness of the family and the distinctness of the persons in the family mirror the Trinity. When God created humanity in his image, he created two editions—male and female. These two were to be joined together as one in marriage. Out of that oneness comes new life. Families were God's great idea, to put persons together and to help us understand who He is. God is the Father of the Lord Jesus, and God the Son is the Son of the Father, and the Spirit is the one who holds the two in love. All three are persons, and yet their unity is fullness of life.

Human families reflect the difference and the unity in the very nature of God, and each family has the possibility of pointing beyond itself to the One who created all families, the One in whom all life is found, the One in whom all love is found. Every family that belongs to Christ and is led by the Spirit for the glory of the Father cannot help bearing spiritual fruit, and that family becomes a doorway of grace through which other families can come to know eternal life. "And this is eternal life, that they would know you, the only true God and Jesus Christ whom you have sent" (John 17:3). We are named for Him, and in His image our families are created! What joy and hope!

Paul's prayer continues: "He would grant you, according to the riches of His glory, to be *strengthened with might* through His Spirit in the inner man, *that Christ may dwell in your hearts* through faith..." (italics mine). I used to think that these two things, strengthened with might and the indwelling Christ, were two separate requests. First, Christians need to be strengthened, and second, Christ needs to dwell in our hearts.

Now, I believe that verses 16 and 17 go together. In order to be in-dwelt by a person of the Triune God, our souls must be strengthened. We were created to be in-dwelt, but the fall has shattered the unity we were intended to know with God. We walked out of fellowship with God, and our souls became weak and lifeless without the invigorating, life-giving Spirit. Such we are without His presence in us and will continue to be without His indwelling presence.

In Jesus Christ, God and man dwelt together in perfect unity. Human persons are made for God; we are created to be inhabited by Him. The hypostatic union pictures for us this reality. We will never be like the God man Jesus, but we are created to be in-dwelt by His Holy Spirit. In the Father's love and mercy, He proved that there is no incompatibility between human nature and His own nature. We were created for Him. We were not designed to stand alone, and our very persons are incomplete without His infilling Spirit.

Knowing our strengthlessness, Paul prays for believers who have received the Spirit. He asks that they would be strengthened in their inner spirits, so that Christ could come and dwell in them through faith. Even after salvation, a strengthening needs to come into our hearts to create enough space for Christ to come and dwell. We are without power and weak, and Christ is life itself. Christ described it as "new wine needing new wineskins" so that the old did not explode. Unless the Spirit comes and strengthens us and gives us a new spirit, our old selves cannot hold the richness and glory of His presence. We must be remade, renewed and restored. But our God is able to make us into a new creation. "Therefore if anyone is in Christ, he is a new creation; old things have passed away; behold all things have become new" (2 Corinthians 5:17). "For in Christ Jesus, neither circumcision nor uncircumcision avails anything but a new creation" (Galatians 6:15).

We must be strengthened, enlivened and prepared for His coming. Having the life of God in us through His Spirit is not a gift to be taken for granted. Our whole body, soul, mind and strength must be given to make a home for God in our souls. "You shall love the Lord Your God with all your heart, with all your soul and with all your strength" (Deut. 6:4).

As the Holy Spirit strengthens our bodies, minds and souls for the indwelling Christ, He roots us and grounds us in His love. His love enables us to comprehend with all the saints what is the width and length and depth and height. In order to comprehend His love and live in His love, we need to be rooted and grounded in His love. We need to accept it and build our lives on it, and the more we know of His love, the more we will come to know.

Jude 24 has become one of those foundations of God's love for me. The translation of the Greek captures the heart of God's saving love. "To the one who is able to keep you unstumbling so you can stand before his glory blameless in jubilation. To the only God our Savior be glory and greatness, power and dominion." A day is going to come when the Lord Jesus will present me before His Father, and I will stand in the presence of all holiness and goodness and power with Jesus. He will keep me "unstumbling" and blameless, and when I stand before the Father I will be jubilant.

In my imagination, I can hear his voice saying, "Here she is, Father! Isn't she lovely?" I will have no fault before the Father if I am with the Son, and my joy will be jubilation. One scholar has said, "This is a dancing word."

When we stand before the Father in the Son, we will be radiant with joy.

As I thought on this, I comprehended in a new way what it meant to have a Savior. Our Savior will keep us and then present us to the Father without fault, and our joy in Him will be complete. Hebrews 12:2 speaks of Christ's joy in us as well. He endured the cross because of the joy that was set before Him, and that joy is to have His loved ones with Him. Having a Savior has become the most beautiful reality in the world.

In Christ Jesus, we are rooted and grounded in this love, and He enables us to understand this new life of love. His presence teaches us the width and length of reality which is His unending love. His presence in our lives and in our families enables us to comprehend the depth and the height of the love of Christ that passes our knowledge. His personal presence strengthens us in our inner spirit, gives us faith to be indwelt, helps us comprehend God's redeeming love, enables us to know His love ourselves, and allows us to be filled with all of God's fullness.

In his book on Joshua, F.B. Meyer writes, "There is a great difference between the strength which may be supplied from without and that which is assimilated within....There are many ways in which the holy soul derives strength from without. It is buttressed by remonstrances and appeals; by providences and promises; by the fear of causing grief; and by the incitement of passionate devotion. But if these were all, they would be insufficient. We need to have within ourselves the strong Son of God; to know that the Mightiest is within us, working through us, so that we, even as he, can do all things."

My five-year-old son had a particularly naughty day. As I tucked him in bed, I seriously talked to him about loving Jesus and allowing Jesus to help him with his obedience and attitude. We prayed together, and he asked Jesus into his heart.

The next day was even worse, and his behavior was so bad that I said, "Isaiah, you can't act like this. Jesus is living in your heart now, and he doesn't want you to be disobedient."

Looking down at his little chest and then back up at me he said with all seriousness, "Mama, I think He left." Recognizing that something had gone seriously awry with my explanation of spiritual life, I had no idea what to say. I stopped to ask Jesus what to do.

Later that night, as we said our prayers, Isaiah said, "Mama, I want to ask Jesus into my heart again." Expecting to have a good discussion and then pray together, I sat down on the edge of the bed.

To my surprise, Isaiah pulled the covers over his head and lay there quietly for a moment. I had no idea what he was doing. All of a sudden, he popped out with a shining smile on his face and said in a loud voice, "Mama, He said yes! He said yes!"

He had prayed under those covers, and Jesus had said to his five year old heart, "Yes, I will live in your heart." He didn't have to pray that prayer again. Jesus did come to live in his heart, and we knew that Jesus loved Isaiah and Isaiah loved Jesus.

The personal presence of Jesus is the key for our children, and we want them to come to know His presence in our homes so they will be accustomed to the sound of His voice and the light of His face. They will know His strengthening hand in their inner spirits as they walk with him. He will speak to their hearts and communicate His presence and comfort to them. We can create a space and be a doorway for Jesus Christ, the King of kings and Lord of lords to come and meet open and hungry hearts.

CHAPTER 3

The Million Dollar Gamble

"I trust in your unfailing love. My heart rejoices in your salvation. I will sing to the Lord for he has been good to me!" (Psalm 13:5-6).
Read Ruth 3.

Christian women are required to take risks! Life is never an easy path of relationships, ministry, profession, and family. Each day requires juggling, wisdom, patience, endurance, and gambles. Passing on a passion for Christ is not something that comes without struggle or without risk or without giving one hundred percent to Jesus. Loving Jesus with all of your heart requires that everything in life be directed to Him and be for Him and be done through

Him. It requires a whole heart, a determined will and an open spirit to His indwelling presence.

Even though I am not a fan of horse racing, I love the movie *Secretariat* because of the courage of Penny Chenery, Secretariat's owner. After her father's death, her brother decides to sell Secretariat for 6 million dollars to pay the inheritance tax. Secretariat has already been named "Horse of the Year," but he has yet to win any leg of the Triple Crown.

Determined not to sell him, Penny invents an outrageous plan. She goes to one of the wealthiest horse owners and asks him to buy a share in Secretariat. If Secretariat does not win all three legs of the Triple Crown, she will refund his million dollar investment and the money paid by any other investors. If he wins, her farm will be secure. If he loses, she will forfeit everything.

Before the Kentucky Derby, Penny participates in a press conference and someone asks her, "Penny, how much pressure are you feeling from your investors right now?" She replies with a smile, "Well, it's like every other all or nothing multi-million dollar gamble that we housewives make every day."

Multi-million dollar gambles made by housewives reminds me of Ruth. Ruth has become one of my favorite stories of a woman who passed on the passion. Her gamble is motivated by her love for another. She comes from Moab, hardly the heritage you would expect for a mother of Israel, and yet she becomes a major player in God's redemptive story. She comes into God's story with nothing but openness, and she contributes a son in the ancestry of the Lord Jesus. Her story is a promise that all the people of the world are included in God's salvation story. She makes a gamble and chooses to live in the light of the other world—the world she has only glimpsed through the seemingly tarnished witness of her mother-in-law.

In the part of the story recorded for us, Naomi does not have many good things to say about Yahweh her God. In fact, she tells Orpah and Ruth to return to their own homes for the "hand of the Lord has gone out against me."

Later in Bethlehem, Naomi tells her neighbors, "the Almighty has dealt very bitterly with me. I went out full, and the Lord has brought me home again empty...the Lord has testified against me." Orpah sensibly returns and makes no million dollar gamble, but Ruth is different. She has seen something of the light that shines from the other world that she does not want to let go, and so she decides to be a boundary dweller. She leaves her family, her country and her gods to accompany her mother-in-law to a new land and a new God.

Her attachment to Naomi is complete and final. She will not ever return to Moab; she chooses to live among the Israelites, even as an outsider, content to be where Naomi is. Here is her first gamble. She leaves all she has formerly known behind.

To live on the boundary between two worlds always requires a courageous choice to leave behind the comfortable and familiar. Choice means limitation. We have to set our face if we are to be boundary dwellers. Giving your life to live between God and our world always involves sacrifice, and it always involves a determined choice to live in between.

"In between" means that we never exactly belong. Ruth was a Moabitess all her life, and her willingness to leave behind her past and begin a new life did not mean that she always felt at home in Israel. It means that we don't feel at home (yet). As long as we are part of God's redemptive story and plan, we must be content with a certain homelessness.

Hebrews 11 is filled with the stories of boundary dwellers. "In between" also means that we are not quite comfortable. Perhaps we feel hurried and pressed. Being part of God's story means that we live with stress and tension. The world is in need of a Savior, and we want to be part of His operations in the world. It requires His courage and His strength. It is never comfortable. Of course, Ruth was not comfortable leaving behind all that she knew, but she was determined to follow Naomi and live in light of her (even slender) faith.

Ruth makes another gamble. She goes out to work the fields and gather grain so she and Naomi have food. As she lives with the Israelites, she sees the genuine kindness in the people of God. She and Naomi are cared for as she goes out to gather grain in the fields. She is not harmed, and as she works hard she knows safety and protection. Ruth is willing to work hard and live hand to mouth, but Naomi has other ideas.

In Ruth 3, Naomi concocts a seemingly crazy scheme, although in retrospect we know the Lord led her plan. Naomi instructs Ruth to go to the threshing floor and lay down at the feet of Boaz, putting herself at his mercy. Ruth has a choice. She has already left behind her family and her country. She has worked hard to provide for this ailing mother-in-law, and now she is asked to make herself vulnerable to a man in hopes of his providing for them.

Will she risk it? Or will she willingly live a life of mere sustenance so that she does not have to take another risk.

I love Ruth's courage. Her attitude seems to be, "I have nothing to lose, so I am going to go for it." Thankfully, she does, and in the middle of the night, Boaz awakens with the realization that a woman is lying at his feet. "Who are you?" he demands. "I am your servant Ruth," she answers. "Spread your garment over me for you are a Redeemer."

This verse has become one of my favorite prayers. Some translations use *kinsman redeemer* and others have *family redeemer* to translate the Hebrew word. The Brown-Driver-Briggs Hebrew lexicon indicates that the Hebrew word means *to be the next of kin (and as such buy back a relative's property, marry his widow, to be an avenger, deliverer, kinsfolk, purchase, ransom, redeem.)* Ruth's request means she is asking Boaz to play the role of rescuer for Naomi by marrying her. Ruth is bold in her risk-taking. She is aware of her need, opens herself to Boaz, and receives Boaz's redemptive response.

First, Ruth recognizes her deep need. She knew that she had no way to take adequate care of Naomi financially or emotionally. She needed someone beyond herself to meet the needs of this mother-in-law whom she loved. Unwillingness to recognize need would have meant poverty and despair for Naomi and Ruth, but honest awareness of need was the greatest avenue for God to come.

Often we believe life just requires a little more juggling, a little more work, a little more creativity. Arrogantly, we think we would have the capability of success if we just had the right resources, the right personnel, the right program, the right job or the right family. We don't realize our need for a Redeemer, even after salvation.

Recognizing our need for the Lord's anointing and His power in our lives for a holy heart and for a fruitful life is the first requirement of being filled with the Spirit. Fruitless and frustrating ministry can be an indication that we are not moving in the Spirit's power but in our own.

This realization should not produce despair but joy. We need Him! The need is not an indication of our own inadequacy, but of our identity. We were made to be completed in Christ and to find our life in Him. If we can learn to run to Him when we are young, the running will become more natural as our bodies weaken and our capacities decrease. "They that wait upon the Lord shall renew their strength." As we come to Him, we find in Him all that we need.

Ruth came to Boaz willingly, and scripture gives no indication of fear or uncertainty in her. She exposed herself to the possibility of humiliation, but she was single-minded in her mission. Her need was greater than any fear she might have felt. When she uncovered his feet and lay down, she offered to Boaz her life, her future, her family, her relationships, her reputation and her security. That night, Ruth was going to be either accepted or rejected – her whole life waited under that garment at the feet of Boaz. She determined not to move until an answer came.

Full surrender calls for this same willingness to come and lay our lives open before our Redeemer in humility and openness without anything held back. In the upper room, after the resurrection, the disciples came together to pray, rejoice and wait for the promise of the Father. They kept coming, kept waiting, willing for the Risen Lord Jesus to have all of their lives. Into the open and trusting hearts of the disciples, the Holy Spirit came with fire and power.

Into the open and trusting heart of Ruth, God poured all His love as well, and then He included her in the redemption story of the world. What she would have missed if she had backed away in fear? Our hearts cry to be part of God's story in the world, to be included in His plan for redeeming billions of lost and dying souls. Openness and trust are the hallmarks of a surrendered heart, and a surrendered heart is one into which God can come.

So, I find myself regularly praying to the Lord Jesus, "Spread your garment over me for you are my Redeemer. I am unable to handle the responsibilities and needs of life. Take me under your protection and be my Rescuer God." I think that God welcomes this openness and request for His care.

Boaz' response to Ruth is a window into God's heart. Boaz welcomes Ruth with a blessing. She is a poor, widowed foreigner, and he is a wealthy, influential chosen one, yet his first word to her is "Blessed." Perhaps the one thing that keeps us from full surrender is our fear of God—what will He make us do? What will He make us give up? Will He embarrass us?

Learn a lesson from God's man, Boaz. God welcomes all who come to Him in openness and faith. He will not turn any away; He will not reject; He will not destroy. Boaz welcomed Ruth, and he called her 'blessed of the Lord.' Then he says, "You have shown more kindness at the end than at the beginning."

The word for *kindness* in Hebrew is *hesed* which is a word unique to the Hebrew language and almost always used of God for His people. This word is the covenant love word between a greater one and a lesser one, and Boaz applies it to Ruth as to the greater one. He receives her request as an honor and a privilege which reveals the heart of this man. Then he goes on to explain this honor: "You have not gone after young men whether rich or poor."

Here, I think is the heart of holiness. We have the absolute privilege of showing *hesed* to our God when we do not go after any other—whether young or old, rich or poor. How do we minister to the heart of God? We do not go after any other! We recognize our need of Him, come to Him in openness and trust, and receive the provision of His love and His Holy Spirit.

The serpent attacked Eve's trust in God at precisely this point. He tempted her to go after another by suggesting to her that God was withholding something good from her—something that she could simply reach out and take for herself. Her sin began as a doubt in her mind that led to distrust of her God and Friend. That distrust quickly became disobedience as she considered her options and reached out her hand to take the fruit. When she did so, her disobedience immediately began to put distance between herself and God.

This lie of the evil one is still around and is still convincing women to get out of the boundary life and on to a side track where we attempt to make life happen for ourselves. The temptation may be to something that appears good—like the fruit. "Wouldn't you like this for yourself?" Then when the woman of faith begins to doubt that God has given her all she needs, she reaches out her hand and begins to break the relationship she has with her Savior. A wholehearted believer keeps believing God is good, and refuses the lie that He is withholding something from us. We must continually affirm His goodness, provision and love. He is our Kinsman Redeemer, and we are under the cover of His garment.

Unfortunately, this temptation can also manifest itself as fear. Perhaps we are not reaching out for something, but we are paralyzed to believe that our God is good and will keep providing for us, and we retreat into fear. This fear can become paralyzing when life does not work out as we expected it to, and God does not perform for us like we thought He would. When the temptation comes to doubt God's goodness and take life into our own hands or retreat into ourselves, we must go on the offensive and declare the truth recorded in Scripture about who our God is.

First, our God is for us, and he has good plans for us. He is *pro nobis* as the early Christians used to say to each other in the marketplace. God is for us. Psalm 56:9 says it well, "When I cry out to you, then my enemies will turn back; this I know because God is for me."

"For behold I bring you good tidings of great joy which shall be to all people. For unto you is born, this day, in the City of David, a Savior who is Christ the Lord...Glory to

God in the highest and on earth, *peace, goodwill* toward men!" (Luke 2:11, 14). "What shall we say to these things? If God is for us, who can be against us? For I am persuaded that neither death nor life, nor angels nor principalities nor powers nor things present nor things to come nor height nor depth nor any other created thing, shall be able to separate us from the love of God which is in Christ Jesus our Lord" (Romans 8:31, 38-39).

Boaz' openness to Ruth, his concern for her well-being, and his desire to become her protector gives a radiant picture of the heart of God toward us. He welcomes us. He wants us to be well in Him, and He desires to be the one to whom we will go for protection and care.

Second, our God wants to be our covering or shelter.

"I will abide in your tabernacle forever. I will trust in the shadow of your wings" (Psalm 61:4).

"Peace, I leave with you. My peace I give to you. Not as the world gives do I give to you. Let not your heart be troubled, neither let it be afraid" (John 14:27).

"Deliver me, O Lord, from my enemies, for in you I take shelter" (Psalm 143:9).

"As the Father has loved me, I also have loved you. Abide in my love!" (John 15:4).

"The Lord will be a shelter for his people and the strength of the children of Israel" (Joel 3:16).

As Ruth talks with Boaz, she finds herself in a new relationship, one in which she still does not know the ending. But his next words prove to her that her million-dollar gamble has been worth the risk. He reveals to her the security of her position. "And now, my daughter, do not fear. I will do for you all that you request." Living on the boundary means we stand at the doorway between eternity and time, and our lives become an opportunity for others to walk through the door and meet the Savior.

To live such a life, two things are essential. First, we cannot be afraid of our God. We must believe that He welcomes us and loves us, so that we can introduce our children, neighbors, friends, and others to Him. All those around us will know if we harbor fear in our hearts about God's goodness.

Second, we must believe with all our hearts that Jesus is our Kinsman Redeemer. He has spread His cloak over us, and we belong to Him. The burdens that we have been carrying may be laid at His feet, just as Ruth placed the care of Naomi on Boaz. It is safe to give ourselves to our Kinsman Redeemer, so that we can be part of the redemptive story that He is working in the world. Because we belong to Him, we are free to live for others.

My mother has said so many times as she has counseled me and other women, "Full surrender is nothing held back, nothing held onto, nothing between you and Jesus." If Ruth had held part of herself back, she never would have gone to see Boaz that night. If she had held onto her independence or her pride, she would never have asked for his cover. If she had allowed something to come between them, like her inferiority, her embarrassment, her past, or her race, she would never have known his redeeming love.

"Take us under the cover of your wing, risen Lord Jesus, for you are our Redeemer."

For a woman and a mother, this may be the most important prayer we ever pray. As we minister to those around us, we find we are unable in our own strength to save even one. We are unable in our own strength to communicate the Gospel message clearly. We are unable in our own strength to bear the burdens of each day and the daily tasks that seemingly never end. We must have a protector.

When we come to Jesus as our Kinsman Redeemer, He assumes our responsibilities, He receives us with His love, and He puts his cloak over us so that we belong to Him. We will know, our families will know and the world will know that we belong to the Lord Jesus Christ. Any mother who wants to pass on the passion for Christ must come under His Lordship, receive His love and accept His provision. When we do, fruitfulness comes into our lives because of Him.

Listen to the precious ending of the book of Ruth. "So Boaz took Ruth and she became his wife, and when he went in to her, the Lord gave her conception, and she bore a son." The women of the village said to Naomi that this son was to be to Naomi a "restorer of life and a nourisher of old age for your daughter-in-law who is better to you than seven sons." That son, Obed, became the father of Jesse, the father of David. Ruth's child became part of the lineage of the Messiah, and Ruth's life was a blessing to all those she encountered. Ruth's delighted contentment in the will of God for her life, her willingness to abandon all out of love for Naomi, and her courage to obey in the face of rejection placed her in the middle of God's redeeming activity for His people and the world.

As Secretariat comes around the final corner of the final lap of the Belmont Stakes to win the Triple Crown, ahead by 36 lengths, the movie goes into slow motion and the verses from Job are read, "He laughs at fear, afraid of nothing...He does not shy away from the sword...He cannot stand still when the trumpet sounds" (39:19-25).

I believe this verse could be applied to any woman, like Ruth, who lives wholeheartedly for God with nothing to lose. May God make us like Ruth, so that our children are part of God's redemptive plan for the world, and we are a blessing and a joy to those around us because we have walked in faithful, courageous and devoted love to our Redeemer.

CHAPTER 4

A Transformed Life

"Christ in me, the hope of glory!" (Colossians 1:27)
Read Luke 22 and Acts 2-5.

I have discovered that family devotions can be excellent opportunities for serious soul work in children and parents. Recently, I read the story of Peter's denial of Jesus to my three children, ages 7-11. Horrified by Peter's betrayal of his best friend, they sat in disbelieving quietness at the end of the chapter. Silence does not happen often at our house, so I quickly realized their distress and said, "Wait! Peter does not always deny Jesus. Let's look at the beginning of Acts." As I explained the coming of the Spirit and Peter's transformation, the Holy

Spirit began to speak to my heart in new ways. In a glorious moment, the heart of the mother as well as the hearts of the children were blessed and encouraged.

We must understand Peter's story if we are to fully comprehend what living a life of faith must be; unless we are filled with the Spirit of Jesus, we will be unable to pass any passion on to our children. Our witness will be diluted and weak, and our children will immediately know our double standard of living. Luke tells Peter's story as Peter journeys through doubt and fear into freedom and life through the coming of the Holy Spirit. This same Holy Spirit offers His life to all Christians that all may live "in Christ Jesus," victorious and content.

Luke gives four graphic pictures of the power of sin and death in the human soul, two from the lives of the disciples and the other two from completely pagan lives. The alarming thing about the four pictures is that they illustrate the same broken and sinful human spirit.

In Luke 22:39-46, Jesus has gone to the Garden of Gethsemane in what could well be His darkest hour. He leaves His disciples with these instructions, "Pray that you will not be overcome with temptation." Then He goes away and pours out His heart before His Father. When He returns, He finds His disciples sleeping. *Overcome with exhaustion*, they rest while Jesus wrestles, fighting the greatest spiritual battle ever fought. Luke indicates that the disciples were sleeping because of sorrow; they felt the tension of the moment, and Luke implies that they knew something was going to happen even if they did not understand what it was. Instead of watching with Jesus for one hour, they sleep. These disciples had the opportunity to stand by Jesus while He interceded with the Father, while He threw Himself to the ground and prayed. He asked them to watch with Him, but they could not.

Only the indwelling Holy Spirit can enable us to watch with Christ for one hour. When we are tempted to be overcome by fatigue, sorrow or fear, the natural inclination is to block it out and sleep or turn our minds off and try to relax. Only in the coming of the Holy Spirit is strength and courage given to enter into the prayers of the Lord Jesus. After the coming of the Spirit of truth, all disciples have the privilege of kneeling beside Jesus as He intercedes with the Father, and instead of prayer becoming a reflection of our inner turmoil, He can pray His prayers through us.

Luke paints the next picture in verses 56-59 as Peter creeps into the courtyard after Jesus' arrest and warms himself by the strangely cold fire. Peter has followed Jesus at a distance, and that distance brings disaster. He has sat down among the crowd when he needed to stand alone, as close to Jesus as possible.

Quickly, a woman recognizes Peter as a follower of Christ. Angered, he responds, "Woman, I don't even know the man!" Overcome by fear, Peter denies the name of the one he loves. Peter denies Jesus two more times; the first time he denies Jesus to a servant girl, the next two to men around the fire.

Only Luke records Jesus' reaction to Peter's denial. "Immediately while he was still speaking, the rooster crowed. And the Lord turned and looked at Peter. Then Peter remembered the word of the Lord...so Peter went out and wept bitterly" (Luke 22:60-61).

Jesus turns to look at Peter, seemingly more interested in what was happening in the courtyard with Peter than He was with His own trial. Jesus responded to Judas this way as well when Judas comes to betray him in the garden. "Will you betray the Son of man with a kiss?" Jesus' seems more brokenhearted about Judas' betrayal than about His being betrayed. The look of Jesus to Peter in the courtyard stirred Peter's memory, and the words that Jesus had said broke Peter's heart. The soldiers and servants must have wondered as Peter jumped out of the circle around the fire and ran out of the courtyard. Perhaps they could hear his cries from outside the courtyard as he wept out his remorse.

Luke presents the third picture in chapter 23:6-8. When Jesus is taken before Pilate, he gladly sends Jesus to Herod for prosecution because Jesus is a Galilean. "Herod was delighted at the opportunity to see Jesus, because he had heard about him and had been hoping for a long time to see him perform a miracle."

Herod, *overcome by curiosity,* attempted to manipulate the Savior of the world for his own pleasure. He was more interested in a phenomenon than in the person of Jesus. This may be the great temptation of our day. In our "techy" world, we gladly trade our birthright for the quickest and coolest experience, and our children will face this same pressure for instant gratification and the tyranny of the next new experience. Herod's self-centeredness was legendary, and in the end it destroyed him as he took for himself honor reserved for God alone. Herod had had an opportunity to respond to the light of Jesus, and he threw it away and chose his own darkness.

The fourth event occurs after Herod sends a silent Jesus back to Pilate, and Pilate says to the crowd, "Nothing this man has done calls for the death penalty, so I will have him flogged, but then I will release him" (Luke 23:15-16). With a cry of outrage, the crowd demands the death of Jesus, and Pilate, like a weary parent with naughty children, is overcome by pressure and gives in to their demands to pacify them.

The disciples and Peter respond to Jesus' arrest remarkably like Herod and Pilate; they are all overcome, whether by temptation or curiosity, fear or pressure. The followers of Christ exhibit no more power to do the right thing than the pagan rulers. But the story has only just begun, and Luke narrates Peter's experiences after the resurrection and the ascension. Unlike Herod or Pilate, the resurrected Lord comes to Peter and to the disciples. They have seen the living Christ, and they wait for the promise of the Father.

When in power and glory the Holy Spirit comes and the Father's promise is fulfilled, the Holy Spirit pours His life into the disciples. The life of God indwelling these 120 men and women effects a joyful transformation. Immediately, Luke illustrates this reorientation by giving four pictures from Peter's life.

First, instead of slinking around behind the crowd, Peter boldly steps forward in front of a large crowd and shouts. "Listen carefully." Then he reveals the Gospel while explaining the writings of the prophets (Luke 2:14ff). Illumination and truth have replaced fear and doubt.

I love Acts 2 because we so clearly see the transformation that the coming of the Spirit brings in the life of Peter. He is filled with the living presence of God's Holy Spirit, and immediately he and the others begin to proclaim God's good news in other languages. Then, when confusion comes to the people, Peter steps up and clearly articulates to this Jewish audience that Jesus is the Messiah, prophesied about by David and the prophets. The coming of the Holy Spirit had been foretold by the prophet Joel, and Peter weaves all this together in order to proclaim that salvation is in the name of Jesus.

Peter's message is perfect for his audience, and the Holy Spirit uses it to save 3,000 that day. I wonder if Jesus had explained these things to the disciples before His ascension, and when the Holy Spirit comes, the disciples are able to verbalize it to representatives from all over the world. The mocking of the crowd turns to repentance and then to rejoicing as they receive the promise of God (Acts 2:38).

When filled with the Holy Spirit, a passion for God's Word begins to grow in our hearts. The pieces begin to fit together and the greatest thrill becomes seeing how God's Word makes sense of our lives and our families' lives.

Secondly, the name of Jesus assumes center stage in Peter's life. Around the soldiers' fire, he could not identify himself with the name of Jesus, but now that name has become his only treasure. Peter gives to the crippled man what he could not offer to the servant girl. Peter and John, full of the Holy Spirit, go to the temple to pray. They meet a lame man who asks for money, and Peter's response reveals the change in his soul. "Silver and gold I do not have" (a common theme among the people of God) but what I do have I give to you: "In the name of Jesus Christ of Nazareth, rise up and walk."

When Peter took the lame man by his hand, his feet and ankles received strength, and he leapt and stood and walked into the temple. Strength replaced weakness, walking and leaping replaced sitting and begging, and belonging and worship replaced alienation and despair. How did Peter account for this transformation? He says to those at the temple, "The name of Jesus has healed this man...Faith in Jesus' name has caused this healing before your very eyes."

When the Holy Spirit comes, the name of Jesus takes on incredible power because He is the source of all life and the center of all reality. The Holy Spirit puts Jesus in His proper place in our lives, our hearts, our families and our world. In our homes, the name of Jesus must have center stage if the passion for Christ is going to continue generation after generation.

The next picture comes in Acts 4:23-31; Peter the sleeper has become Peter the warrior. After the arrest and then release of Peter and John, all the disciples unite to pray. No longer overcome by temptation, their prayers for boldness and courage bring the Holy Spirit into their midst, and he shakes the place in which they sit. This is one of the most astounding changes to me.

Before the crucifixion, the disciples could not pray for one hour and they were powerless to pray. When the Holy Spirit comes, the prayers flow out of their hearts and minds with power, anointing and boldness. "'Now, Lord, look on their threats, and grant to your servants that with all boldness they may speak your word.' And when they had prayed, the place...was shaken, and they were filled with the Holy Spirit, and spoke the word of God with boldness."

As carriers of the presence of Jesus into a lost world, we must be filled with the Holy Spirit so we have the courage, strength and anointing to pray God's prayers for His people and for the world.

Finally, evil is overcome by the life of God in Peter. When Ananias and Sapphira lie to the Holy Spirit, Peter confronts the lie and proclaims God's judgment. Evil is not allowed to harm the fellowship of believers. Ananias and Sapphira come in to meet Peter after they have consented together to lie to him about the price of the land they had sold and the money they were giving to the church.

Peter, full of the Holy Spirit, knows their deception, and he asks, "Why has Satan filled your heart to lie to the Holy Spirit?" It is not against Peter or the church that Ananias and Sapphira have sinned but against the Holy Spirit of God. Peter becomes the doorway through which God's judgment comes because he is living in the fullness of God through the Holy Spirit. Peter's fear of others and concern for himself has vanished in the fullness of God's Spirit in his life.

Peter's life is transformed when he receives the Holy Spirit. Holiness is receiving the life of God through the power of the Holy Spirit. The Holy Spirit gives Jesus center stage in our lives as we surrender all of ourselves, all of our lives, all of our fears and all of our hurts to Him. As we wait and ask the Holy Spirit to fill us, the life of God will flow abundantly into our hearts.

In the Incarnation, God and man came together in Jesus our redeemer, fulfilling the Father's original plan for His creatures to be filled with His presence. In the giving of the Holy Spirit, God comes to dwell in us and we become "partakers of the divine nature" (2 Peter 1:4). Human creatures were made for this unity, and we will find abundant life only when we live "in Him." No longer must we be slaves to temptation, fear, phenomena or pressure. The sleeping, slinking, fear-filled Peter before the cross is not the Peter that God made him to be. As we open our hearts to receive the Holy Spirit, He will give Jesus center stage in our lives and set us free to be overcomers, living with courage, openness and faith.

CHAPTER 5

Living 100 Percent for Jesus

"In the fear of the Lord there is strong confidence, and His children will have a place of refuge. The fear of the Lord is a fountain of life, to turn one away from the snares of death" (Proverbs 14:26-27).
Read Isaiah 49:5, 15-16; Isaiah 65:24.

As we receive the Holy Spirit into our lives and ask Him to make Jesus center stage in our families, we will be surprised and delighted when He comes to meet our children. The greatest thrill of being a parent is creating a space for the Spirit to come and meet with your children. Welcome Him into your home. Create time for Him, and make Him the top priority, and then when He blows where

He will and comes into your home, listen for Him, watch for Him (John 3:8). When He comes to speak to your children, you can watch, pray and marvel at the ways of God with the little ones in your home.

I remember when my children were much younger and we were talking to them about what it meant to be a follower of Jesus and ask Him to live in your heart. One day, I walked down the hall to the bedroom, and I thought "Jesus is here, and He is speaking. But He has not come to speak to me. He has come to speak to my children. I have the privilege of welcoming Him in and allowing Him room to work and time to speak."

We must be sensitive to the Spirit and be willing to slow down and listen when we sense He is talking to our children. We dare not waste the opportunity to introduce our children to Jesus. We watch and wait as He calls them and draws them and loves them!

Extremely tired, I made my way down the stairs to my son's bedroom to tuck him in for the night. After we read our Bible story, he asked, "Mommy, what does it mean to love Jesus with 100 percent of your heart?" My mind felt fuzzy, but I knew he was serious and Jesus was speaking to him. So, praying as I went, we began to talk about what it meant to give to Jesus everything. Finally, he said, "Mama, I think I am only 75 percent." It took me only a moment to grasp what he was saying, and then I said, "Would you like to belong to Jesus 100 percent?"

"Yes, I would." We stretched out on his bed and began to pray together that his whole heart would belong to Jesus, and he laid out his life before Jesus and gave to his Savior all his desires, wants, likes and dislikes. When we had finished praying, he said, "I belong to Jesus 100 percent."

Our greatest mistake may be in thinking that our children are too young to be all God's or that they couldn't possibly understand. Children know what loyalty and devotion are. They can understand what it means to give your heart to someone 100 percent, and they know that they do not want to live with bad thoughts and hurtful actions. They want freedom from sin as much as adults too, and we must believe that it is possible and present it to them as the glorious possibility of the Gospel. Peter's life was transformed by the infilling of the Spirit, and I know that our God is still in the business of giving His Spirit to those who ask.

One of my children's favorite verses is, "What man, if his son asks for bread will give him a snake? Or if he asks for a fish will give him a scorpion? If you then, being evil, know how to give good gifts to your children, how much more will your heavenly Father give the Holy Spirit to those who ask?" Our children know that fathers give good gifts, and they can know that their Heavenly Father will give His best gift to them as well. The Father will give the Holy Spirit to our little ones when they ask.

One night, my son yelped, and my husband realized the dog had run into his room and jumped up onto his bed to be snuggled. He went in to sort things out. After he sent the dog downstairs, hugged our son and tucked him back in bed, a little loving voice said, "The best thing in the world is having a daddy!" Our heavenly Father is better than any earthly daddy could ever be, and He will give Himself to any child who asks for Him. We have the privilege of setting the stage, creating the space for our children to meet their Heavenly Father and to be filled with His Holy Spirit.

The night we read the story of Peter's denial, I knew God had come to speak to our children. As we talked about Peter and his temptations and his inability to live boldly for Christ, our living room became quieter and quieter. Even as my energetic seven-year-old settled down and gave the story his full attention, my nine-year-old curled up against me on the couch and was absolutely still.

My eleven-year-old listened intently, and all of a sudden I knew the Holy Spirit had entered our family room, and He had captured the attention of my children. Carefully, I continued as he brought an illustration to my mind. "Remember Papa's story about his trombone?" I asked quietly.

Their great grandfather found Jesus when he was 13 years old at a camp-meeting, and three days later at that same camp, he heard a preacher speak on being filled with the Holy Spirit. That night, around a wooden altar in Georgia, he surrendered all he had and all he was to Jesus Christ. His heart was so filled that night with glory and with love that he stayed up all night rejoicing and loving Jesus.

But then he had to leave camp and go home, and when he went home, he went to a high school where he only knew two other born again Christians. He had played trombone in a band before he had received Christ and been filled with the Holy Spirit, and now the band players came and asked him to play again. Papa knew that Jesus did not want him to play in that band—not because music is wrong, but because he would have to go to places and play music that Jesus would not like. "How can I explain this to my friends?" he prayed. And then he knew, and when his best friend came to ask him to play he had his answer. "We are best friends, aren't we?"

"Sure, Dennis."

"You know I would never do something that would cause you pain or hurt, right?"

"Sure, Dennis. So what?"

"I have found another Friend, one who is even closer than you. His name is Jesus, and I know that it would hurt Him if I stayed in the band. I don't want to do anything that would hurt my best friend Jesus."

I explained the story further. "After Papa found Jesus and received the Holy Spirit in his life, he had power to stand up and obey what God told him to do just like Peter did. On our own, we have no power, but the Holy Spirit can fill our lives, so we have power to do what He wants us to do."

Silence in my living room. And all of a sudden I looked over, and my seven-year-old was crying. "Would you like to give everything to Jesus and ask him to fill you with His Holy Spirit?"

"Yes," he whispered. We began to pray together a simple seven-year-old prayer, but tears coursed down his face as he prayed to give to Jesus his whole heart—all of Jesus for all of him, and then he asked Jesus to fill him with the Holy Spirit.

When we finished praying, we cheered and celebrated and then the boys snuck away, but my daughter did not leave my side.

"Honey, would you like to pray?" She nodded.

We began to pray. First, she gave Jesus everything she has—all of herself, all of her friends, all of her interests, all of her possessions, and then she began to pray, "Jesus, I give you my desk and my dresser..." When she said "dresser" I looked over at her thinking she was joking, but the tears were streaming down her face too. She went through her little room in her mind, giving Jesus every part of it. We held our hands out together and offered all she was and all she had to her Savior.

Then I felt the Spirit nudge my heart, "Let's give Jesus all your fears."

Immediately she began to name several fears, and we held them up to Jesus. Then He whispered to my heart, "Let's give Him all your hurts." In her nine-year-old heart, she had hurt, and she offered it to Jesus too. "Now, I said, "Let's ask Jesus to fill you full with His Holy Spirit." She prayed and asked to receive the Holy Spirit. He came! I know He came because after we prayed she radiated peace and joy, and we turned to Acts to read the stories of Peter and she couldn't put her Bible down. Her heart had been quickened to His Word. We found a journal for her and went over the stories of Peter, and she began to faithfully read her Bible and talk to Jesus. A quiet and awestruck Mommy prayed that night over her children.

In His Word God has given us some precious promises to claim for the next generation. These verses from Isaiah are perfect prayers to pray over our children.

"'As for Me,' says the Lord, 'This is my covenant with them; My Spirit who is upon you, and My words which I have put in your mouth, shall not depart from your mouth, nor from the mouth of your descendants, nor from the mouth of your descendants' descendants,' says the Lord, 'from this time forth and forevermore'" (59:21).

"All your children shall be taught by the Lord, and great shall be the peace of your children. In righteousness you shall be established; you shall be far from oppression, for you shall not fear; and from terror, for it shall not come near you" (54:13-14).

"For I will pour water on him who is thirsty, and floods on the dry ground; I will pour my Spirit on your descendants, and my blessing on your offspring; They will spring up among the grass like willows by the watercourses" (44:3-4).

CHAPTER 6

A Divine Moment

"Look to me, and be saved, all you ends of the earth! For I am God and there is no other...To me every knee shall bow and every tongue shall take an oath. He shall say, 'Surely in the Lord I have righteousness and strength'" (Isaiah 45:22-24).
Read Acts 10.

God passionately loves the whole world! We have the joy of sharing His passion for Europe, Africa, Asia, Australia, North America, and South America. His love encompasses every country, every family, every child. He has no desire for only a few children; He wants the whole world to be saved! As we grow in our faith as families, we begin to share this passion for the world. What joy to carry God's world and His burden on our hearts together.

Scripture gives such a riveting account of the early church and how the Gospel spread throughout the known world. One of our privileges and joys as Christian parents and caregivers is to instill in our children a passion for seeing God's Word go out to the whole world. We have the awful tendency of wanting to make sure that our families are cared for without too much extra pressure or stress and then we leave the rest of the world in God's care.

But God is looking for people who will join Him in the salvation of the world. In fact, He told His disciples to bear this burden before He ascended to the Father. "All authority has been given to Me in heaven and on earth. Go, therefore, and make disciples of all the nations, baptizing them in the name of the Father and of the Son and of the Holy Spirit, teaching them to observe all things that I have commanded you; and lo, I am with you always, even to the end of the age" (Matthew 28:19-20). So how do we pass on to our children a passion for God's world?

The story of Cornelius has helped me so much. God has a plan for the world, and after Pentecost, He began to put it in motion. Peter is right at the heart of this profoundly significant moment. He is on the rooftop of his friend Simon's house, who is a tanner and lives by the sea. From the rooftop, Peter can probably see the sea and hear the sound of its waves. It is around lunchtime, and Peter is praying. Rather suddenly in the middle of his prayer time, he becomes hungry and wants to eat. While they are preparing his food, he falls into a trance.

Peter's vision unfolds as a sheet out of the sky. Inside the sheet are all kinds of animals that are unclean: wild beasts, creeping things and birds. Then Peter hears a voice, "Rise, Peter; kill and eat." Peter's response sounds more like the old pre-Pentecost Peter than it does the new Peter, "Not so, Lord!" Peter has never eaten anything unclean, and he informs the Lord of his ceremonial cleanliness.

Then the voice speaks again, "What God has cleansed you must not call common." This happened three times, and then the sheet of animals returned to heaven. As Peter pondered this vision, a knock came at the door, and three men from Cornelius' house—three Gentile men—stood at the gate asking for Peter. In God's mercy, He does not even leave Peter on his own to interpret the dream. He tells him, by the Spirit, the men are coming and seeking him. Listen to His specific instructions, "Arise…Go down…Go with them…Doubting nothing for I have sent them" (Acts 10:20).

Previously in Caesarea, a town about 30 miles away, another man had been praying. He had been praying about 3 o'clock the day before, and he had seen a vision. This man's name was Cornelius, and he was a Gentile who feared God and was devout. Cornelius saw an angel of God coming to him with a message. "Your prayers have been answered and your alms have come up for a memorial before God. Now send men to Joppa, and send for Simon whose surname is Peter. He is lodging with Simon the tanner whose house is by the sea. He will tell you what you must do." Cornelius did not waste a minute after the angel departed, he called two servants and a faithful soldier from his staff, explained to them what had happened, and sent them to Joppa to find Simon Peter.

The men knock at the door. Peter obeys the vision and goes downstairs and meets the men whom God has sent. He invites them into the home as his guests. This is the first indication of his obedience. He willingly welcomes the Gentiles as his guests. The next day, Peter and other believers in Jesus from Joppa accompany the three men to Caesarea.

After the 1970 revival at Asbury College in Wilmore, Kentucky, Dennis Kinlaw who was President of the College at that time said, "Give me one divine moment where God acts, and I say that moment is far superior to all human efforts of man through the centuries." God is in charge of our time. A seemingly trivial afternoon prayer and lunch time transform into one of the most important moments in human history.

One moment God is appearing to Cornelius through an angel and then at just the right moment, he speaks to Peter, and the world is never the same. It is in the in between moments when God comes and transforms lives and human stories. He wants to have full control of all of our in between spaces. Luke gives incredible detail about this story, and I think it is to emphasize its importance in God's economy. When God wants to accomplish His purposes, He makes sure it is done, and nothing hinders His plan.

God is able to break us out of our boxes and prejudices. He is able to do something new in a believing heart, and He tenderly guides and works until we can see clearly. God does not leave Peter on his own to interpret his dream according to his own ideas; he comes to Peter and speaks to him, giving specific instructions. God wants His will to be done, and if we are living in the Spirit, He is not going to let us miss His perfect will just like He is not going to let His perfect moment pass us by.

When Peter hears God's voice, he obeys. He opens himself to this radically new idea and acts on it immediately. He does not send Cornelius' men to the inn down the road while he thinks about this. He hears God's voice, and he invites the men into the home where he is staying and welcomes them.

When Peter arrives at Cornelius' house, Cornelius is waiting for him. Cornelius takes God and His word seriously. He has called his friends and family together to meet him. When he greets Peter at the door, he falls down at his feet and worships. He has no understanding of what he is doing, but he knows that this one has been sent from the God he worships, so he is prepared to worship Peter as well.

Of course, Peter will have none of that. "Stand up! I myself am also a man." Then Peter explains to Cornelius his own situation, and it how it is that he has come to be in a Gentile home. Peter seems to be understanding that this is a crucial moment, but he still has not put all the pieces together for in the next breath he asks, "For what reason have you sent for me?" Peter still does not clearly comprehend that he is to tell these Gentiles about Jesus.

When the Holy Spirit begins to break open our boxes and put us in new situations, it comforts me that he works with the understanding we have. He does not chide Peter for not having full understanding. Peter's willingness to obey meant that God had an opportunity to bring the whole situation into the light. Cornelius explains how God came to him and had him send for Peter. "Now therefore, we are all present before God, to hear all the things commanded you by God."

Finally, God can accomplish His purposes in and through a willing heart. Peter does not understand at first that God wants the Gentiles to know about Jesus, but God keeps ordering circumstances and conversations until he comprehends God's larger plan. And then, Peter realizes this most joyous truth. "I perceive that God shows no partiality. But in every nation whoever fears Him and works righteousness is accepted by Him."

God shows no partiality; what an incredible revelation to come to the people of God. The Jewish people had their identity in the fact that they were chosen, and now God says that whoever calls on Him will be accepted. A great door is being opened up in the heart of the Gospel message as the salvation of Jesus is available to all men and women.

While Peter explains the gospel message which started with the Jews but has spread to include anyone who believes in Christ Jesus, the Holy Spirit comes. He falls upon this large group that has heard the Word of God. Instead of expecting this move of God, the Jewish people with Peter are astounded because God also poured out the Holy Spirit on the Gentiles. Nothing was held back, but all was given including God's Holy Spirit.

The gifts of the Holy Spirit were also given as Cornelius' friends and family begin to speak with tongues and magnify God. So first God gives the visions (one to Cornelius and one to Peter), then the welcome (Peter welcomes the men, and Cornelius welcomes Peter), then the message (it began with the peace of God given to Jews and ended with 'whoever believes in Him will receive remission of sins), then the Holy Spirit (the Gentiles receive even as the Jews have received the Spirit), and finally baptism (identification with Jesus for Gentiles as well as Jews). Peter answers, "Can anyone forbid water, that these should not be baptized who have received the Holy Spirit just as we have?" And he commanded these to be baptized in the name of the Lord Jesus.

We have the privilege of introducing our children to the work of God around the world. We must be intentional about this to expand their minds beyond the narrow sphere of our individual family lives and help them realize that God is at work in the world. Wherever He has a willing heart, that one can become a doorway for the Gospel to spread into other places. There are so many ways to expose our children to God's work in the world. One way is to invest in missionaries.

Our community has many missionaries coming and going, and my children love hearing their stories. One missionary lady told my boys a story about Colombia. Some of the guerrilla fighters were attacking innocent people, and the Christians knew they were going to die unless Jesus protected them. She described it like this: "It was like Jesus let down a force field in front of his children, and the bullets could not hurt them." She went on to explain how God protected and rescued them. Jesus—as our force field—became an important bulwark in the faith of my sons. Jesus can protect us. He is powerful and is at work right now in places around the world!

Give your children opportunities to hear the stories such as this. Invite missionaries into your home. Let your children give to the missionaries and support them with their own money. Keep a missionary journal with prayer cards and pray your way through the book.

At Lent, our family felt led to pray around the world. We have a prayer map that divides up all the countries of the world into 31 days so we can pray around the world in a month. In preparation for Easter, we decided to pray around the world that Jesus would prepare His world for the resurrection and prepare our hearts for what He wanted to do. Every night, we spread the map on the floor and each child took two or three countries. If we knew information about the countries, we would share what we knew. If a specific country was in the news, we would talk about what was taking place, and then we would pray through the countries.

As Easter approached, I knew that God had used it to keep the world on all our hearts. Easter is for the world, not just for our family. This is so important for our children to know. We prayed for Christian parents and children. As our prayer guide suggested, we prayed for "open doors," "open minds," "open hearts," and "open heavens."

I did not even realize what a profound impact our prayer time was having on our family. One night, my seven-year-old fell into bed before prayer time. As the rest of us prayed together that night, we gave Isaiah's countries to his Daddy to pray for. In the morning, Isaiah woke up and came running to me, "Mama, we forgot to *pray!*"

Quickly, I reassured his little heart. "Don't worry, Isaiah. We prayed together, and Daddy prayed for your countries." Peace filled his heart and joy shone in his eyes. He was carrying God's burden, and He didn't want to let it drop. These little ones are ready to share the passion in God's heart for the world.

Jeremiah 5:1 has become one of our favorite verses to show that each one of us can make a difference in our world. "Run up and down the streets of Jerusalem; search high and low, and see if you can find one person who does justice and seeks truth, then I can save the city."

Finally, as we pray, we must listen to the Spirit. One way to pray may not always work. Children need to have variety, and so we need to keep asking the Lord Jesus how to share His burden for the world with our children. Of all the resources we have available, I find the best and most interesting for our children is from the Word itself. When God has spoken to the parents' hearts in quiet time, and the parents share those insights with their children, the children respond most readily and eagerly.

CHAPTER 7

Glory of the Gospel

How utterly astounding and significant. I am not a creature of chance but was formed in the womb by my loving heavenly Father to be His child and my purpose in life is to please and obey the one who gave me life. (my mother's Bible)
Read I Corinthians 12:4-20 and I Thessalonians 2:11-12.

Watching our children begin to be part of God's redemptive plan in the world is one of the thrills of life. Even as young as elementary school, children can begin to carry the world on their hearts and want to give of themselves to reach others for Jesus. Perhaps we have been so accustomed to going to church and being spoon-fed the gospel, we forget it is something that we must appropriate in our lives. Let us be part of building the Kingdom of God in the world. As families we must join together to reach the world for Christ. Our children can become part of God's redemptive story. In fact, God's answer to the problems of the world has always started in a child. It is His way to use the children to reach the world.

This all came to my mind as I was praying with my children. After two of my children prayed to be filled with the Holy Spirit, one of them immediately became burdened for a specific classmate. I suggested that he could find out this friend's favorite candy, and we could take him a treat. Several days later when I had forgotten all about it, he said "Mom, we need a Snickers." Even then, I did not make it a top priority, but he would not let me forget. So we bought the Snickers and he took it to school. Then we went through the Wordless Book together, and I gave him a copy to take to school to share with his friend. The wordless book is a book that uses colors to explain God's plan of salvation.

At the breakfast table the morning before school, he practiced explaining the salvation message with me while his brother and sister looked on. This little one had a mission and was single-minded about it. When he arrived home at the end of the day, I asked, "How did it go?"

"Well mom, I went through every page with him. Other kids came around to see what we were doing, and I just told them, 'Get Away! We are learning the Wordless Book.'" The next week he had invited his friend to church, and at the end of that first night at church when I went to pick them up, he said, "Mom, he is ready."

"Ready for what?" I asked. (How can moms be so slow?)

"To ask Jesus into his heart," he responded incredulously. "I asked him if he wanted to, and he said yes!" I looked down at his friend who was smiling up at me as if to say, "What are we waiting for?" So I said, "Why don't we go into the sanctuary and pray together?" And we did. The three of us knelt by the pew and prayed for this little precious child to be forgiven and receive Christ into his heart.

God can burden a child's heart and enable that one to follow through until God works. My son doggedly took every step to get this one saved by Jesus, even if sometimes his technique could have been a little more gentle. As I watched him earnestly and seriously pray and love and drag his friend into the Kingdom of God, I found myself asking some questions.

What is the mark of the Spirit in a child's life? Is it always the same or does the Spirit move differently in each child? How can I encourage my children to be sensitive to the Spirit and encourage these gifts that He has placed within them?

One of the extraordinary things that I have found as I have prayed over my children and considered each one with their different personalities is that each child has a spiritual gift. When a child has given his heart to Christ and the Holy Spirit has come to dwell in that child's heart, he has a sensitivity to the Spirit that increases as he grows in grace. That spiritual gift begins to burn more brightly and becomes a joy to watch.

As I have thought about my three children, I have been amazed by their uniqueness when it comes to walking with Jesus. Some children may have the spiritual gift of loving, and their acts of service and kind ministrations are an indication of the Spirit at work in their lives. This child may reach out to others with comfort, encouragement, kindness and patience. This child will offer a winsome witness that will draw others especially as our world becomes more and more broken and fragmented.

Other children may have the spiritual gift of standing firm. This gift of "standing" may be manifested in some of our most reserved children, but when the pressure comes to do something that would hurt Jesus, they will not budge. This gift is absolutely essential if we are going to raise up leaders for the Kingdom of Jesus in the world. Other children may have the gift of evangelism, and if given the encouragement and the opportunity, they will lead their friends to Christ. We must train our children to reach out. We need to teach them ways to share their faith and verses in scripture to share with their friends. We need to be willing and ready—more ready than I was—to help direct and pray when our child is reaching out.

Each child of God, no matter how small, has been given a gift of the Spirit. The mother's job is to discern the voice of the Spirit and encourage the gift that has already been given. If I look at my child who has the gift of loving and say, "We need to really reach out and love this little hurting one" my child blossoms. If I say, "You need to tell your friend about Jesus," that child freezes even though she loves Jesus with all her heart.

I don't mean for one minute that we should not teach all our children to share their faith or to love others with Jesus' love or to stand firm in the face of trial. All our children need to be able to do all of these to be a soldier for Christ, but we can encourage the gift God has given so that the joy of witnessing or being a witness is experienced by our children. A child who has given his heart to Jesus and received the Holy Spirit should not be made to feel guilty for feeling uncomfortable with another approach.

In the educational world, we are always hearing about different types of learners and how the classroom should encourage every style of learning so each child can thrive. In a similar way, in the Kingdom of God, each child has been given a gift to use for Christ, and each one should be praised and affirmed for his or her place in God's heart. We all have a special role to fill in God's economy, and I think it will help our children if they know that they are already fulfilling it as they live out their lives in love for Jesus.

Learning your child's gift can be a thrill of delight and discovery as you watch to see how He works in each ones life. His creativity is endless, so His gifts in our children will be varied and different. I have only given you three as an example. Look for others: encouragement, teaching, helping, speaking, leading, praying, creating. As we strengthen the hands of our children to give their witness, I believe all areas in our children will be fortified and built up. What a privilege and joy!

II Thessalonians 1:11-12 is a glorious promise and prayer to pray over our children and our families. "Therefore we also pray always for you that our God would count you worthy of this calling, and fulfill all the good pleasure of His goodness and the work of faith with power, that the name of the Lord Jesus Christ may be glorified in you, and you in Him, according to the grace of God and the Lord Jesus Christ."

Four prayers to pray and four promises to believe for our families. First, the unbelievable truth is that God might count us worthy of this incredible calling. How amazing that God could count us worthy to be part of spreading His good news; only the blood of Jesus makes this possible. Our families live in the overflow of our Savior's love and that love enables us to be part of His plan for the world.

Second, God will fulfill his good pleasure in us as families and as individuals. He will make us pleasing to Him; we don't have to be striving to please Him. That is His business, and He will fulfill His pleasure in us.

Third, He will accomplish His work in us with power. Sometimes we need to know that He is going to do His work in spite of our mistakes, accidents or even failures. We belong to Him, and He will complete the work He has begun in us. Finally, Paul prays that the name of the Lord Jesus would be glorified in us and we would be glorified in Him. God's grace can bring glory to the Lord Jesus through our lives, and when Jesus is glorified we participate in that glory (John 17).

God counts us worthy of this calling. We have the privilege of participating in His work.

God will fulfill in our families His good pleasure.

God will accomplish His work with power.

God will glorify the name of the Lord Jesus through our lives and our families. He will glorify us with the Lord Jesus.

CHAPTER 8

Nothing to Lose

"Lead me, O Lord in your righteousness because of my enemies. Make my way straight before your path" (Psalm 5:8).
Read Joshua 1.

Passing on the passion for Christ to the next generation means that we must be filled with God's Holy Spirit, living in Him and letting his life flow out of us for others. Because of this, we must not be content to stay still. We must be willing to be part of God's redemptive story for the whole world. Recently, I have been reading *The Hobbit* to my eleven-year-old son. I am not sure who has enjoyed it more; I think it is I because the adventure seems to fit a life of faith. Bilbo Baggins finds himself on an adventure he did not want to take, with dwarves he does not particularly enjoy, lacking all the comforts of home, and yet he finds himself marching onward, visible or invisible, to conquer the dragon and find the treasure. At the very beginning of his journey, when things just had become uncomfortable, he thinks to himself, "I wish I was at home in my nice hole by the fire, with the kettle just beginning to sing!" "It was not the last time that he wished that!" the narrator of the story exclaims.

Christians are pilgrims on a journey, not hobbits around the fire. Hebrews 11 explains our state, "These (men and women of faith) all died in faith, not having received the promises, but having seen them afar off were assured of them, embraced them and confessed that they were strangers and pilgrims on the earth. For those who say such things declare plainly that they seek a homeland. And truly if they had called to mind that country from which they had come out, they would have had opportunity to return. But now they desire a better, that is, a heavenly country. Therefore God is not ashamed to be called their God, for he has prepared a city for them" (11:13-16).

Like Ruth, we are pilgrims, on a journey. If Ruth had thought about Moab, perhaps she could have returned, but she had gained a new desire, a desire for a better country. No matter how many times we wish that we could sit by the fire and settle in, God has another home for us, and He is calling us to come higher up and deeper in. We must be willing to live in the uncomfortable middle of an adventure with each day given to Jesus for His will to be accomplished and His plan to be unfolded.

Like the children of Israel, we must be willing to journey into the Promised Land and actually claim the promises of God for us, our children, our families and our world. We must begin to expect God to answer the prayers we are praying, and seriously and diligently take Him at his word.

What is a promised land? We wish sometimes it was a land flowing with milk and honey, where the battles are all fought and the rest is already won. However, just like the Hobbit's adventure, the Promised Land is full of battles to fight, giants to kill, and hard work to do. To be honest, no wonder the Israelites didn't fully conquer their inheritance. Without the Holy Spirit's indwelling presence, how could they? Life is a battle even if circumstances are relatively normal, but in this day—nothing is normal—not even the weather.

Passing on a passion for Christ to the next generation requires that we stop every once in a while and take a look at our own hearts. It means facing the fears of moving forward in God's plan—or fears of inadequacy, failure, and the unknown. These fears have to be met, not denied, and then they have to be given to Jesus for His healing and His redemption. I know for sure that I don't want to spend forty more years or even one more day wandering in the wilderness—I am ready to go into the Promised Land. But like the Israelites, I must stop on the edge of the Jordan and listen to the voice of God.

The book of Joshua begins after the death of Moses. I am so prone to miss the obvious, but when I read Joshua now, this simple fact grabs my attention: *God speaks.* God is still speaking even after the death of Moses. He speaks into the vacuum created by the death of the greatest man who had ever lived. He speaks to Joshua, the son of Nun, the new leader of the people of God.

How many times have we forgotten that He speaks? He speaks when there is a leadership transition. He speaks into our need, our loneliness and our void. He has spoken to our grandparents, our mentors, our parents, our friends, but He is waiting to speak to us too!

What does He say to Joshua? First, He acknowledges a new reality. "Moses, my servant, is dead." I wonder how many times that horrifying thought had been ricocheting through the mind of Joshua. "Moses, God's servant, is dead! Moses, God's servant is dead!" And now, God comes and acknowledges the finality of this new stage in the history of his people.

But God does not stop with the past; He turns his attention to the future of His people. God is always interested in our future. Whatever He has done for us in the past, whatever He has done for our fathers and our grandfathers, our mothers and our grandmothers, He is ready to act for us now in this moment. And so He says to Joshua, "Now therefore..." I love these two words. Now is the time for action. The moment has come that God has been waiting for. Now therefore, he has a plan for His people. Oh, blessed plan of God. To wander in the wilderness for so long, to spin your wheels year after year, to wait on God's time can be a painful time of learning and faith building. But oh, the glorious day when God says, "Now...." Now is the time that I want to do something in your heart, your family and your circumstances. If He is saying, "Now," do not be afraid. Going forward with Him is where the victories are won and how the Gospel plunges forward.

"Arise, go over this Jordan, you and all this people, to the land that I am giving to them—the children of Israel. Every place that the sole of your foot will tread upon I have given you, as I said to Moses." God's first instructions to this new leader are basic. Although Joshua is not young, he is new to this position of authority, and God gives him simple directions.

First, God says "Arise." Following God always requires us to go forward, sometimes on our knees, sometimes trembling, but always moving in His direction. Remember God's words to Moses at the Red Sea, "And the Lord said to Moses, 'Why do you cry to Me? Tell the children of Israel to go forward.'"

Or to Ezekiel, "Son of man, stand on your feet, and I will speak to you. Then the Spirit entered me and set me on my feet, and I heard him who spoke to me" (Ezekiel 2:1-2).

Or to Daniel, "O Daniel, man greatly beloved, understand the words that I speak to you and stand upright" (Daniel 10:11).

God wants us to be ready, not just curled up on the couch or snuggled in our bed praying or relaxing. When He is ready to move, we need to be ready. The meaning behind the Passover is this readiness. God is about to act, so make your sacrifice. "And thus you shall eat it: with a belt on your waist, your sandals on your feet, and your staff in your hand. So you shall eat it in haste. It is the Lord's Passover" (Exodus 12:11).

Many years later, another Passover meal was eaten, not in Egyptian huts, but in an upper room. God was about to set the world aright; He was coming to redeem and to save, and so, perhaps without knowing what they were doing, they ate this Passover meal of anticipation and readiness.

Also, God says to Joshua, "Go over this Jordan." The fathers and mothers of this people had been over another sea, but this new generation had never experienced the parting of the waters. Before we cross into the Promised Land, God wants to hold back the mighty waters so we know that He has opened the way. If we are in a position where we do not need Him to open any doors or hold back any rivers, we are probably not in the position He wants for us. He is interested in proving His power to His people, and it was not enough to have proved it to their parents. I love this word.

I am a fourth generation Christian, and how to pass on the passion is a question I live with all the time. I want to know the risen Lord Jesus for myself and not because my parents, grandparents and siblings know Him. I am surrounded by others who show me Jesus every day, and I have said to Jesus many times, "Lord, I will be content with how you choose to reveal yourself to me even if you choose to reveal yourself to me through the grace in other people. I will be content to live with the experiences of you and the reality of you that I know." Guess what! I am not content any more. I am claiming this promise, "Open your mouth wide, and I will fill it" (Psalm 81:10).

I am no longer content with seconds. I need to know His presence in my life, my heart, my anxieties, my fears, and my circumstances. When I was a small child and my father was away on a trip, I would sometimes sleep in the big bed with my mama. She has told me many times that I wanted to sleep as close to her as possible. If she tried to be more comfortable and turned her face away from me, I would say to her with childish astonishment, "But Mama, we aren't nose-to-nose." I want to live nose-to-nose with the Son for the glory of the Father through the power of the Spirit, and I want to be as hungry and desperate for Him as if I had only just heard His name. I have no hope except in Jesus, and my prayers this year echo Moses,' "Show me your glory!" (Exodus 32:18) and "If your presence does not go with us, do not bring us up from here" (Exodus 32:14-15). He's the one that I want and the one that I need. YHWH wanted to reveal His powerful guiding presence to the new generation of Israelites, and He wants to reveal Himself to us as well. Whether it is the Red Sea or the Jordan, He wants us to trust in *Him alone!*

Further, God says to Joshua that He is *giving* the land *to the children*. I am interested in two words in this line. God is giving the land. The children are receiving the land. They are not responsible for this gift; they are only to hold out their hands and receive what the Father is giving. Giving is one of the key themes of the Old Testament, and Deuteronomy is filled with references to God giving this land to His people.

One of my favorite verses from Deuteronomy is 1:6 "You have dwelt long enough at this mountain...See I have set the land before you; go in and possess the land which the Lord swore to your fathers—to Abraham, Isaac and Jacob—to give to them and their descendants after them." God's promises to the fathers will be fulfilled for the children. God is giving His people—not to Moses or to Joshua—a gift, and He expects them to be ready to receive it.

Joshua is entrusted with this people to help them receive their inheritance. He is not receiving it for himself —to make a name for himself. He is a mediator of the inheritance of God. He stands between God and the God's people as one who enables them to go forward into the Promised land. In this way, Joshua prefigures the Lord Jesus, who mediates our salvation and our entry into the promised land of life. "He is the Mediator of the new covenant, by means of death, for the redemption of the transgressions under the first covenant, that those who are called may receive the promise of the eternal inheritance" (Hebrews 9:15).

Every Christian has been given the precious gifts of God's life and redeeming love. Once we have received God's gift of grace, we become mediators to help others receive their inheritance. Nowhere is this more important than in the home. Our calling is to help others receive their inheritance from God the Father.

However, Joshua is not a pawn in God's hand, a mere tool to accomplish God's purposes. God's faithfulness to Joshua has lasted for more than 70 years, and He is going to continue His trustworthy care of His servant. He gives Joshua a breathtaking promise that applies to Joshua and the people, "Every place that the soul of your foot will tread upon I have given you as I said to Moses." This promise would be unbelievable except that the guarantor is God. God, in his mercy, has given Joshua a foundational promise as he starts out on this journey. God gives His assurance that this conquest is from Him and God will accomplish His purpose through Joshua.

When God comes to His servants and begins to speak, He gives them something to stand on—a word, a promise, an encounter. As we go forward into the full purposes of God for ourselves and our families, we can trust that He will give us the assurance we need. Four chapters later, before the fall of Jericho, God not only gives His promises, He comes with His presence and declares that He is the Commander of the Lord's Army. Joshua is not alone but is under the command of God.

Next, God gives the boundaries of the Promised Land. From the wilderness and Lebanon as far as the great river Euphrates, all the Hittite land and down to the Great Sea, this is the land God will give to the Israelites. God has a specific place for His people, and He has chosen the boundaries. Life's possibilities only seem limitless to the very young, and as we grow we realize that life has built-in limitations.

God had a land for His people—not the entire world, but one specific land. He has a land for us as well, a specific place where we are to live and accomplish the purpose He has for us. He does not want us to be always looking past the boundaries He has set for us. His borders are good, and the battles to be fought within the boundaries He has established will be enough to keep us busy and complete in Him. His will is specific but not limitless. It is the limits that show His love and show the tender care which He lavishes on each one of His children. Are we bound by circumstances? Let us not seek to be lifted out of our circumstances but set free within the boundaries He has placed us.

In the book of Acts, we see again God's specific directions to His people. "Arise and go south along the road which goes down from Jerusalem to Gaza." This enabled the Gospel to go into Africa for the first time. Again, in Acts 16:9, "And a vision appeared to Paul in the night. A man of Macedonia stood and pleaded with him saying, "'Come over to Macedonia and help us.'" This vision enabled the gospel to penetrate into Europe for the first time. Whenever God is claiming new ground for Himself, He gives specific and limited directions. We must be willing to follow His leading and live within the borders He establishes!

Joshua 1:5 says, "No man shall be able to stand before you all the days of your life; as I was with Moses, so I will be with you. I will not leave you nor forsake you!" Next, God gives a three part promise. First, Joshua will be able to stand before his enemies and accomplish this task given by God.

Second, and even more precious, God gives a promise of His continual presence. God wanted Joshua to know that His presence would be with him even as it had been with Moses. God was neither diminished nor divided after Moses' death, and He assures Joshua of His continued faithful direction.

Finally, God gives the most precious ringing promise of all. A personal promise to Joshua that God would not leave nor forsake him as he journeyed forth. I do not believe I am taking God's promises seriously enough. We read the promise and say, "Okay great." And then we turn around and live in fear, afraid to take the next step of faith much less to cross the Jordan and conquer the Promised Land. God's promise to Joshua on the verge of the Jordan encompassed all Joshua needed to go forward. No enemies shall stand before you. God's past faithfulness continues with this new leader, the future is wide open because God will not leave His people or forsake them.

God commands Joshua to be strong and of good courage. Joshua must divide this land God promised to Abraham, Isaac and Jacob as an inheritance to their children. Joshua is working with God to fulfill the promise God made to the patriarchs of the children of Israel. God asks His servants to come alongside and help Him accomplish His plans for His people, and when we are fear-filled or timid, God is not able to fully accomplish His purposes.

One of the joys of this journey of faith is the people whom God connects. I happened to have a conversation with a godly woman, and she said, "The next time I see so and so, I am just going to ask her, 'Honey, have you ever met Jesus? If not, I can introduce you to Him." Then the woman looked at me with joy and said, "After all, I have nothing to lose.'" Those words gave me courage.

After that conversation, I found myself in a store with an opportunity to witness. "Well?" the Holy Spirit nudged me, "You have nothing to lose!" Then He helped me give my witness. Later that day, friends showed up rather unexpectedly, and I felt another nudge, "Cricket, you have nothing to lose!" This one was harder, but I knew the Spirit helped me turn the conversation to Christ and give my witness.

Two days later, I was taking home a little neighborhood boy from church. He had been on my heart, and I wanted to ask him if he knew Jesus and what it meant to be His follower. That same sweet voice whispered to me, and I knew I had nothing to lose and this little boy had heaven to win.

The Holy Spirit came into our car, and my children hushed and began to pray as I witnessed to this small child about the Lord Jesus. Jesus came into our minivan, and we were able to come around our friend and love him and support him in Jesus' name. Don't be afraid!

I could entitle my journey of faith as "The Salvation of a Timid Soul." I asked Jesus into my heart with my mother when I was four years old. I knew that I belonged to Him, but as I entered middle school and then high school, my soul began to struggle and yearn for peace, security, hope and discipline.

One day after a fight with my mom, I ran down the street. I can still remember hopping up and down on the curb—angry and desperate. "Can't you do something more for me?" I raged at the sky. Apparent silence, and then I looked up at the heavens in my pain and said, "Father, I give you three years to prove yourself to me and in my life. If you can't do something for me, I'll...I'll...I may just walk away from you!"

I knew that God was good and I didn't want Him out of my life, and I knew I was throwing down a challenge and I wasn't brave (or maybe stupid) enough to give God an ultimatum. To be honest, I didn't really believe He would work so fast that I would immediately see changes in my heart. I knew how much I needed Him. So in my fear of losing Him, my fear of myself, my fear that I could never be transformed, I gave him three years. Timid—even with God.

Three years later, I found myself in Paris, France. My sister was sleeping next to me on a queen size mattress laid out on the floor. We were visiting my aunt and uncle, missionaries to the outskirts of Paris. Quietly in my heart, I was praying and worshipping Jesus. He had become my comfort, my friend, my shelter, my Savior, and my beloved.

All of a sudden I realized it was the anniversary of my challenge! Three years earlier I had cried out to my heavenly Father, and He had met me with His love, His grace, His precious presence. I knew that I was loved by Him and I loved Him with all my heart. I slipped out of that bed and knelt in worship. My loving and patient God had transformed my heart and life. He had become my rock and my fortress. He had navigated painful and difficult days; He had provided for me and cared for me. He had given me so many love gifts to prove Himself to me, and the most precious was the assurance of His presence. From that moment, I was His and He was mine. "My beloved is mine, and I am his" (Song of Songs 2:16).

Perhaps you don't feel brave and courageous. You may be like me. Timid soul, don't pull back. Come to meet Jesus face to face. Cry out to Him! He will answer you! As you go forward in faith, you will find that He will come to meet you. You don't have anything to lose, and you have love, life and joy in Jesus to find! His promise for all of us is His presence. "Do not be afraid, nor be dismayed for the Lord your God is with you wherever you go" (Joshua 1:9).

CHAPTER 9

Facing the Giants

"Now therefore give me this mountain" (Joshua 14:12).
Read Joshua 14:1-15:20.

As we help our children and families claim their inheritance, we will have giants to face. Claiming our inheritance as followers and lovers of Jesus is an exciting and challenging journey. The giants in the Promised Land come unexpectedly and take us by surprise, but there are ways we can prepare ourselves for the battles that will inevitably come. Sometimes it helps to simply review the stories of those who have gone before—who claimed their inheritance successfully and did not waver at the promise of God, but believed Him and saw Him accomplish His purposes in their lives. It will help our children to read the stories of those who had courage under fire because of the presence of Jesus in their lives.

Caleb is one of those who claimed his inheritance after 40 years of waiting. In fact, as one of the 12 spies which Moses sent out from Kadesh Barnea, Caleb had been dreaming about his inheritance for a very long time. When he and Joshua went out as spies, they came back triumphant believing that the Lord had already given the land into their hand because of His promises. "Let us go up at once and take possession for we are well able to overcome it" (Numbers 13:30).

But the rest of the spies talked disparagingly. "The land through which we have gone as spies is a land that devours its inhabitants, and all the people whom we saw in it are men of great stature. There we saw giants (the descendants of Anak came from the giants), and we were like grasshoppers in our own sight, and so we were in their sight" (Numbers 13:32-33).

We know the tragic end of that story; none of the men of Israel entered into the Promised Land besides two, Caleb and Joshua. Now Joshua is leading the people to claim their own inheritance, and Caleb has a special inheritance to claim as well. He is not the leader as Joshua is, but God has a special reward for him. In Joshua 14 Caleb comes to Joshua in Gilgal. "Remember, I was 40 years old when we went to spy out the land, and I brought back word as in my heart...I wholly followed the Lord my God." He reminded Joshua that Moses had promised that he could inherit the very land they had spied out—the land of the Giants. Now, forty five years later, Caleb tells how God has kept him for this inheritance. His strength for war is just as great as it was in Kadesh Barnea.

So he makes his request, "Now therefore, give me this mountain of which the Lord spoke in that day; for you heard in that day how the Anakim were there, and that the cities were great and fortified. It may be that the Lord will be with me, and I shall be able to drive them out as the Lord said" (Joshua 14:12). Joshua's heart, I am sure, leapt within him at the courage of his friend. He blessed Caleb and gave to him Hebron as an inheritance. "Hebron, therefore, became the inheritance of Caleb son of Jephunneh the Kenizzite to this day, because he wholly followed the Lord God of Israel."

Caleb's courage came from his commitment to wholly follow the Lord. He had this commitment at the entrance to the Promised Land from Kadesh Barnea, and in 40 years of wandering and in five years of helping others claim their inheritance, he had not lost his commitment to follow God wholeheartedly. He was as determined and hopeful of the conquest now as he had been all those years before. The passion in his heart did not waver, and he did not stop believing in the promises of God. "Now faith is the substance of things hoped for, the evidence of things not seen...Without faith it is impossible to please Him, for he who comes to God must believe that He is and that He is a rewarder of those who diligently seek Him" (Hebrews 11:1, 6).

Caleb's courage did not diminish with age. In fact, I think it increased. He was determined to inherit the land of the giants, the very land that had so terrified the others before. Caleb drove out the three sons of Anak. He promised his daughter to the man who could attack Kirjath Sepher and take it. Othniel, his brother, took this city, and he gave him his daughter Achsah.

Caleb's courage continued to the next generation. Now Achsah had courage of her own. Before she married Othniel, she persuaded him to ask her father for a field. And then she came to Caleb and asked him to give her a blessing and springs of water. Caleb must have seen his own determination and courage in his daughter, for he gave her the upper and lower springs.

A woman who wholly follows the Lord has courage in the wilderness, a courage that does not diminish in forty years of wandering because of other people's sins. What strength there is in this. He can keep us fresh and flourishing even as we bear the sins of others. But a day will come when He leads us into the promised land. If we have wholly followed after our God, our courage will not diminish but increase, and that courage will be passed on to the next generation.

We must remember Achsah when we pray for our children. She had courage to ask her Father for a field and for springs, and he gave to her upper and lower springs of water—more even than she had requested. When we pray for our children, we need to pray expectantly and pray large prayers. Amy Carmichael, a missionary to India, rescued hundreds of girls who were being sold into temple prostitution. She and other followers of Jesus established Donhavur, a place of safety and protection for these little ones. Here are her prayers for the children.

Make them good soldiers of Jesus Christ; let them never turn themselves back in the day of battle.

Let them be winners and helpers of souls.

Let them live not to be ministered unto, but to minister.

Make them loyal; let them set loyalty high above all things.

Make them doers, not mere talkers; make them sound.

Let them enjoy hard work and choose hard things rather than easy. Forbid that they be slackers. Make them trustworthy. Give them grit.

Make them wise, for it is written He hath no pleasure in fools.

Let them pass from dependence on us to dependence on Thee.

Let them never come under the dominion of earthly things; keep them free.

Let them grow up healthy, happy, friendly, and keen to make others happy.

Give them eyes to see the beauty of the world and hearts to worship its creator. Cause them to be quick to recognize "figures of the true."

Let them be gentle to beast and bird; let cruelty be hateful to them.

May they walk, O Lord, in the light of thy countenance.

Her prayer continued, "Let this be the inheritance of these children—the upper springs and nether springs of life." May we claim springs of living water for our children as well, not simply for a happy life but that their lives would count for God's Kingdom.

In reading Proverbs 31, I have found that Caleb's daughter is not an exception. She is simply a woman of faith—a woman who fears the Lord. Proverbs 31:10 says, "Who can find a virtuous wife?" But the Hebrew is actually "a wife of valor." This woman is worth more than jewels. First of all, she brings blessing to her husband. She is trustworthy. Her husband is safe with her and will be blessed because of her. She brings him good all the days of her life. His reputation is safe with her and is better because of her. A wife of valor is also hard working. She willingly works with her hands doing the jobs she needs to do. She cares for the ones for whom she is responsible. She feeds her children and others; she makes clothes for them, and she is loved by them. She is creative and industrious, not paralyzed by fear or fright. She has an inner strength and a discerning mind. She has a loving heart that reaches out to the needy around her. She does not fear hard times for her family. They are well cared for. Strength and honor encompass her, and she rejoices in the future—living without fear. She opens her mouth with wisdom and lives in kindness towards her family and all others.

I used to read this and think "Expectations!" Now, I read it and think "Promise!" However far I am from this woman of valor, the Holy Spirit is at work to fashion me into the woman that makes a difference in her world. The woman who fears the Lord shall be praised, her works shall praise her in the gates, and she shall eat of the fruit of her hands. These are promises to a woman of faith.

As life becomes more challenging, we want to look to other places to meet our needs. Parents are aging and resources might be tight, and we find ourselves shut in by life and circumstances. It is in these moments that we need to come to the Lord Jesus to meet the needs of our hearts. When we come to Him, out of our hearts will flow rivers of living water. I believe that we, like Caleb's daughter, can ask for springs, but our springs are not the upper and lower ones on the field. Our spring is the living well inside of us that only Jesus through His Spirit can give.

When we come to Jesus, and He is enough for us— meeting every need and satisfying every desire— then our lives are free to be a blessing to other people. They will live in the overflow of the Spirit's life in us, and in His life is blessing, joy, peace, strength and grace. So instead of causing fear or anxiety in our children, we can bestow on them blessing and peace by living in the stream of the Spirit every day.

A life of dependence is what faith in Jesus is all about. He does not make us self-sufficient women but radically dependent on Him. Our dependence on Christ to meet every need, fill every moment, encourage every heart, and make us a witness to the world will enable our children, husbands, neighbors and friends to have the opportunity to walk in the overflow.

For Further Study:

"In that day it shall be that living waters shall flow from Jerusalem (or your address)...

And the Lord shall be king of all the earth" (Zechariah 14:8, 9).

"Whoever drinks of the water that I shall give him shall never thirst. The water I shall give him will become in him a fountain of water springing up to everlasting life!" (John 14:13, 14).

"If anyone thirsts, let him come to me and drink. He who believes in me, as the Scripture has said, out of his heart will flow rivers of living water" (John 7:37, 38).

"Along the bank of the river, on this side and that, will grow all kinds of trees used for food; their leaves will not wither and their fruit will not fail. They will bear fruit every month, because their water flows from the sanctuary. Their fruit will be for food, and their leaves for healing" (Ezekiel 47:12).

CHAPTER 10

Joining the Fight

"Help us, O Lord our God, for we rest on you, and in your name we go against this multitude. O Lord, you are our God" (I Chronicles 4:11).
Read Ephesians 6:10-20.

As Christian families we are in a battle, and our children are soldiers too. I used to think that my primary role was to protect them from the battles that were raging around them, but the best thing we can do is equip them to fight in the battle. Passing on the passion means that we have the privilege of asking the Spirit to guide us as parents to train our children in God's battle strategies. Ephesians 6:10-20 has been a wonderful tool to teach our children how to be part of God's battle. When children are confronted with the evil of the world or the temptation to sin in their own hearts and minds, it helps them to know that they have weapons to use to fight back. This has been particularly helpful with my boys! Sitting around the kitchen table one morning, I explained to our children that we are in a spiritual battle, and they are warriors too. Like Lucy and Susan in *The Lion, the Witch and the Wardrobe*, even my daughter took joy in being given a gift to fight back. It has helped my children to learn that our only weapon for fighting back is the Word of God. We have many promises for protection, but when we want to go on the offensive (or are called to claim new territory) it is the Word of God that goes before us and makes a way for us.

So we began to sharpen our weapons, which meant that we began to seriously learn Bible memory verses. First, children need to know that scripture verses are weapons that can be used in times of temptation, fear or trouble. The Word of God is living and powerful, and Jesus used scripture to fight temptation in the wilderness. Second, it is a comfort to children to know that they are not at the mercy of bad thoughts, temptations or the uncertainty of the world around them. Their shelter and high tower is in Jesus, and the way we remain in Him is by living in and through His Word. Third, the verses that speak to a child's heart are not always the verses that we are memorizing. I have found that some unexpected verses really capture a child's heart and mind and become a weapon that he or she can use. My 11-year-old son memorized Isaiah 27:1. "In that day, the Lord with His severe sword, great and strong, will punish Leviathan the fleeing serpent, Leviathan the twisted serpent, and He will slay the reptile that is in the sea." I had come across this verse in my daily Bible reading, and I rejoiced in the triumph of God over evil. I read it to my son, and it became his favorite. God is going to fight the battle, and He is going to win. One day on the way to school, he said it to the rest of us. When I complimented him on remembering it, he said, "Mama, I say it to myself every day!" What are your child's interests and fears? The Word of God can minister to the hearts of our little ones more deeply than we will ever know. We need to immerse ourselves in God's Word so that we can introduce them to different promises that will enable them to stand and fight when they find themselves in the battle.

Psalm 144:1-2 is one of our battle verses. "Blessed be the Lord my rock who trains my hands for war and my fingers for battle. My lovingkindness and my fortress, my high tower and my deliver, my shield and the One in whom I take refuge, who subdues my people under me."

Our God is the God who trains us for the battles that we will have to fight, and He will train our children as we ask Him to. As followers of the crucified and risen Lord Jesus, we must have realistic expectations for the world in which we live. Some times in our comfortable culture, we lose touch with the fragility of life and the depth of pain in our world. When we are confronted with trouble and pain, we shout out accusations at our Heavenly Father. "Why are you allowing this? Why are things not working out? Where are you?" Like the disciples in the boat, we become easily angered when life takes a difficult turn. "Don't you care if we perish?" becomes our cry to the Lord as well. I have been asking the Father to help me have realistic expectations for living in a fallen world. Our world is shattered and broken because of sin, and the effects of sin are going to come to every human life and every human family. So how do we help our children to not be afraid of the battles they will face, but to be ready to face them with courage and strength and even joy?

One wise preacher I heard said, "The only thing worse than a fallen world that doesn't work right would be a fallen world that did work right. That kind of world would be a lie and an illusion." Our world was created by God, and we were made to be completed in Him. When we walk away from the source of our life, we walk into darkness, and when cultures walk into darkness, the darkness can be very deep and penetrating. We must train our children for battle.

Stanley Tam, whose book, *God Owns My Business* has riveted thousands of Christian businessmen, offers two prayers that he prays every morning over his family. The first is a prayer for divine wisdom to meet the needs of the day, to make godly choices and have godly responses. The second prayer is a prayer of protection. Here is what he says: "You only have one enemy. When you become a believer in the Lord Jesus Christ, the evil one has lost you from his family, and he has only one goal – to cripple you and make you useless for Christ. Every morning bind the devil by the power of the Word, the blood of Jesus, and the authority you have in God as a Christian. Name every family member, your home, car, vocation, social life, finances, those with whom you work, etc. Do it out loud. The evil one is not omnipresent! You will begin to see a releasing of the presence and power of Jesus to bring transformation into lives and impossible situations."

The Psalmist also believed that God could keep us in the battle, so he lists all of the ways that God meets us and protects us. He is our lovingkindness, and this is that special Hebrew word *hesed* which is the word for faithful, unending covenant love. So in the middle of the battle, we have the assurance of His faithful and unending love. We are not alone in the battle, and we need to assure our children that they are never alone.

He is also our Fortress. A fortress surrounds; it is a place of safety and security where we are protected from the attack of the enemy. "Be my rock of refuge, a fortress of defense to save me. For you are my rock and my fortress; Therefore, for your name's sake lead me and guide me" (Psalm 31:2b-3). Our children need to know that Jesus surrounds and protects each of His followers. St. Patrick's prayer is my favorite example of this, and my children memorized the chorus one year. The assurance of Christ's presence on every side and in every circumstance and with every person comforted and strengthened us all.

Christ be with me, Christ within me, Christ behind me, Christ before me, Christ beside me, Christ to win me, Christ to comfort and restore me. Christ beneath me, Christ above me, Christ in quiet, Christ in danger, Christ in hearts of all that love me, Christ in mouth of friend and stranger.

Our Savior is also a High Tower. My grandmother used to quote Proverbs 18:10. "The name of the Lord is a strong tower; the righteous run to it and are safe." The safest place for moms, dads and children is in the center of

God's will, and obedience will produce blessing and fruitfulness. Every forward thrust for God brings blessing to our children and parents.

Airports are very familiar to our family; we are always sending someone away and saying good-bye for painfully long times. As our family members head overseas to follow Jesus in Europe and Africa, my father always says, "Remember the safest place is in the center of God's will." And so grandchildren and children can be trusted into the hand of God for His purposes to be accomplished in their lives and in the lives of others. Jeannine Brabon, missionary to Medellin, Colombia, has a famous phrase. "Safety is not in the absence of danger, but in the presence of Jesus." With that as one of her life mottos, she has ministered without fear in some of the most dangerous prisons in the world because of the presence of Jesus.

In the battle, Jesus is also our Deliverer. Psalm 18:1, "I will love you, O Lord, my strength. The Lord is my rock and my fortress and my deliverer; my God, my strength, in whom I will trust." Our Redeemer is not only our strength. He is the rock we stand on, the fortress that surrounds us and the deliverer who goes out before us and fights our battles. Psalm 18 presents a beautiful picture of God coming to the rescue of the one who cries out to Him. "He thundered from heaven, and the Most High uttered his voice…He sent from above, He took me; He drew me out of many waters. He delivered me from my strong enemy."

Our children must know that they can call on Jesus, and He will answer them. Encourage them to see answers to their prayers. Pray about small things and large things, and then keep a record of how God answers their prayers.

When the answers don't come as they are hoping or expect, keep encouraging them to cry out to the Lord. He will answer the prayers of children. He is waiting to prove himself to the next generation of believers. He will not be silent when our little ones pray, and it will be fun to watch how He makes himself known to them.

One of the verses that helps me is 2 Peter 3:14. "Therefore beloved (woman)…be diligent to be found by Him in peace, without spot and blameless." We do not have to force a relationship between God and our children. He will come to them and prove Himself to them, and we can rejoice in it and rest in it.

At night, when my children feel afraid, Ephesians 6 has been a great help. Some nights before we go to sleep, we put on our armor. It goes something like this.

"Okay guys, let's put on our armor. What is first? The belt of truth. Buckle it on. What is true? Jesus loves you (John 3:16). He is here, and He will keep you (Psalm 121). Put on the breastplate of righteousness (Jesus is your righteousness - Jeremiah 23:6). Put your shoes of peace on, so you can share the gospel of peace (John 14:27). Take your shield of faith—we believe in the Lord Jesus. This shield quenches some of the fiery darts of the wicked one? Right? *No!* All the fiery darts are quenched when we say 'Jesus is Lord of me!' (I Corinthians 12:3). Put on your helmet of salvation to protect your mind (Philippians 4:13). Remember you belong to Him. Take up the sword of the Spirit which are all our memory verses."

We say some of our memory verses, and God's Word brings peace to their hearts and assures them that Jesus is with them and will keep them. When of our children was younger, he was having extreme difficulty going to sleep, we started listening to a CD of Bible verse songs. We have been listening to that same CD for a couple of years now, and the whole family can sing every Bible verse on the CD. Those verses come to our minds at the sweetest times for comfort, strength and courage. One night, I was lying in bed feeling anxious, and I thought, "I am going to sing my way through the memory verse CD. I made it through about 8 verses before I fell asleep in His comfort and peace. What a blessing those sleepless nights have brought to all of us.

On her way overseas Amy Carmichael claimed Psalm 59:10, "My God of mercy shall come to meet me!" and Psalm 118:14 The Lord is my strength and my song and my salvation."

Her words about that day remind us of His *enoughness* to meet the every need in our children's hearts. "Let us remember we are not asked to understand but simply to obey. On July 28, I sailed and just as the chill of loneliness shivered through me, a warm clasp came and the long loved lines, 'only heaven is better than to walk with Christ at midnight over moonless seas!' I couldn't feel frightened then; praise Him for the moonless seas, all the better opportunity for proving Him to be indeed the El Shaddai, the God who is enough."

He is enough for every need and for every battle.

For Further Study

II Chronicles 20 is a wonderful chapter to work through with your children.

"For we have no power against this great multitude that is coming against us; nor do we know what to do, but our eyes are upon You" (2 Chronicles 20:12).

"Do not be afraid of this great multitude for the battle is not yours, but God's" (2 Chronicles 20:15).

"You will not need to fight in this battle. Position yourselves, stand still and see the salvation of the Lord, who is with you...Do not fear or be dismayed; tomorrow go out against them for the Lord is with you" (2 Chronicles 20:17).

"He (Jehoshaphat) appointed those who should sing to the Lord, and who should praise the beauty of holiness as they went out before the army and were saying, "Praise the Lord, for His mercy endures forever." Now when they began to sing and to praise, the Lord set ambushes against the people of Ammon...and they were defeated" (2 Chronicles 20:22).

CHAPTER 11

Resting In Him

*"In heavenly love abiding, No change my heart shall fear;
and safe is such confiding, for nothing changes here. The
storm may roar without me, My heart may low be laid,
but God is round about me, and can I be
dismayed?" (*Green Leaf in Drought Time*)
Read John 10.*

Adventures can be exhausting! Our journey into life
with Jesus is no exception. Just as Bilbo Baggins wished for
his Hobbit Hole in the middle of his adventure, so we may
wish for a security that does not change. Life beats
relentlessly and leaves bruises and scars. Our heavenly
Father does not take us out of the battle or out of the trials

of living in a fallen world. As Amy Carmichael prayed, our Father knows we need "grit" to stand in this broken world, so He keeps us in the fight.

The role of a mother does not lessen as her children grow; it increases and her level of faith must increase to meet with the mounting demands that she feels. John 10 has become my refuge when this feeling of exhaustion hits. We may be living in His presence and listening to His voice, yet life still seems to be more than we can handle. We are buffeted on every side, and our bodies, minds and spirits can't keep up with the needs or the demands of the day. We can't form a coherent thought much less think of how we need to pray for our children and train them to be warriors for Jesus.

Paul, the apostle, had moments like these, which gives me great comfort. "We are hard pressed on every side…we are perplexed…persecuted…struck down…always carrying about in the body the dying of the Lord Jesus… death is at work in us." Of course, I have left out the best part of the verse, but sometimes it helps to remember that the trials come not because of some failure on our part, but because God is at work in us and through us. It is He that keeps us from being "crushed, in despair, destroyed." And He frees the life of Jesus to be manifested in our body so that the life of God can work in another. Into these moments of confusion or pain, Jesus our Good Shepherd comes.

John 10 does not begin in a idyllic, pastoral way. Jesus does not say to His disciples, "Don't worry. Everything is peaceful and lovely, so just relax." John 10 begins with the enemy, the one who is climbing in some other way than the right way. Life outside the fold is not safe, and the enemy outside is seeking to snatch the sheep out of the fold. No pretense is made in scripture about that. There are those who would kill and destroy the sheep, but the shepherd enters by the door. Jesus is the shepherd; He is not sneaking in but coming in the front door to claim what is rightfully His. The door is opened to Him, and immediately the sheep hear His voice. When the Good Shepherd comes, those who have been following Him will recognize His voice.

Sitting around the kitchen table for devotions, I talked to my children about John 10. "Don't worry you will know His voice because you belong to Him." I have found that one of the main fears of my children is whether they will recognize His voice when He calls to them. "What does He sound like? How will I know?" they ask anxiously. Here, we find the answer. These are His sheep, and they immediately know His voice. His assurance helps our children have peace that they will not miss His voice or His best. He will make Himself known to them. I am embarrassed to say how old I was before I realized that God could talk to me directly and not go through another family member. What a thrill to begin to hear His voice and to teach our children that they can hear His voice as well.

The other thing my children love is that the Shepherd calls them by name. He knows each one, and we are not just a mass of messy, noisy, bothersome sheep. These sheep are special, and the Shepherd cares for each one. The Shepherd brings the sheep out, and He goes before them. I believe that our God wants us to live like those little dumb sheep. Following our Shepherd, listening to His voice, and staying as close to Him as we can possibly be. When the needs of life are at their greatest, I am finding great joy in saying, "Father, I am a little sheep, sitting at your feet. What do you want to do next? Where do you want to go? You make the next move, and I will follow you." This dependent living takes all of the anxiety and fear out of trying to manage life. We are to please the Good Shepherd, and it does not really matter if any other sheep is pleased with us or not.

Samuel Chadwick said in one of his great sermons, "I do not make my way or find it; I follow Him." Listening to His voice, I move from one activity to the next and from one person to the next and sometimes from one crisis to the next. When He is leading, a light and a glory come into the most mundane tasks, into the most trying relationships, and into the most frightening circumstances. His presence transforms and His wisdom bring life and light.

When Jesus told this parable to the people of Israel, they did not understand. I am not surprised by their inability to grasp this life of dependent living; it is so hard for me to believe that He really does not want me to have it all together. He really does not need me to have all the answers. He really does not desire me to be the center of every show. He has it all together; He is the answer, and He is the center of all that lives and breathes. I live because of Him, and my life is to flow out of Him.

Jesus gives another compelling parable to help them understand the freedom of the life He provides. "I am the door. If anyone enters by me, he will be saved and will go in and out and find pasture" (10:9). Not only is our Savior the shepherd, He is the door. He is the way into every new day. He is the way into every new conversation and every new situation. He is the door through which we enter into life. Salvation comes when I enter through Him. And then I am free to enter in and out and find pasture. He is my way. All provision is made through Him for each day. Every need is met in Him. Psalm 23 makes this so clear. He makes us rest in green pastures and leads beside still waters. He restores our soul and leads us in the path of righteousness. He is the Shepherd who provides pasture.

He is also the Shepherd who provides protection. "The thief does not come except to steal and to kill and to destroy. I have come that they may have life, and that they may have it more abundantly. I am the Good Shepherd. The Good Shepherd gives His life for the sheep." One day as I was thinking of this passage of Scripture and resting in the protection and provision of the Good Shepherd, I realized with startling clarity, that my protection was not easily gained. He gave His life to protect me. He spilled his precious blood, so that I would be free to live in His fold, under His care and His protection. As a little sheep, I wander from my Shepherd. "All we like sheep have gone astray, we have turned everyone to His own way" (Isaiah 53:6). God the Father has laid on His Son all the sins of all His sheep. Perhaps when John recorded Jesus' words about the Good Shepherd, he was thinking about Isaiah 53, and the price that had to be paid so that we could live in His care.

Like Edmund in C.S Lewis' *Chronicles of Narnia*, we have been bought with a price, and we dare not take our redemption lightly. We must live with joy in His presence, as close to our Savior as we can be--content to be where He is and to follow His direction.

When our circumstances press, and pain us, He will sustain us and provide for us day by day and moment by moment. Arthur and Wilda Matthews, as told in *Green Leaf in Drought*, were missionaries in China, and they found themselves under communist rule with ever tightening restrictions on ministry, food, and relationships with the Chinese. Eventually, they became confined to their small, cold house with almost no contact with the people they had come to serve. They claimed Andrew Murray's four anchors for trials, and I think these will help any woman resting in Christ in the middle of the circumstances God has allowed for her.

"He brought me here. It is by His will I am in this strait place, and in that fact I will rest. He will keep me here in His love and give me grace to behave as His child. Then He will make the trial a blessing, teaching me the lessons he intends for me to learn. In His good time He can bring me out again – how and when He knows. So, let me say, "I am here by God's appointment, in His keeping, under His training; for His time."

Christ is our provision and our protection, and we can trust Him and rejoice in Him and in His providential care of our circumstances. He may be weaving so intricate a design in our lives that we can neither see it all nor understand it all, but we can trust Him. As we do, He will open up opportunities for our children and our families. As we trust Him with every child, in every new stage of life, with every new opportunity, and in every relationship, we will find that He is faithful and loving. As we walk in obedience to Him, we will enter His rest and will find that we please Him, and that He is working on our behalf to accomplish His purposes in our lives.

Sisters in Christ, let us go forward, committed to passing on a wholehearted love for our Lord Jesus Christ to the next generation. As we journey with Him further up and deeper in, let's claim His glorious promises. Let us rejoice because He covers our families; He blesses our families and He surrounds our families as with a shield. "Let all those rejoice who put their trust in You: Let them ever shout for joy, because you cover them; Let those also who love Your name be joyful in You. For You, O Lord, will bless the righteous; with favor you will surround Him as with a shield" (Psalm 5:11-12)

And even greater, let us rejoice because our Savior has come, and through His Holy Spirit, He will dwell in our midst and make us His people! "Sing and Rejoice, O daughter of Zion! For behold, I am coming and I will dwell in your midst, says the Lord. "Many nations shall be joined to the Lord in that day, and they shall become My people, and I will dwell in their midst" (Zechariah 2:10-11).